Landmark Visitors Guide

North Wales
& Snowdonia

Colin Macdonald

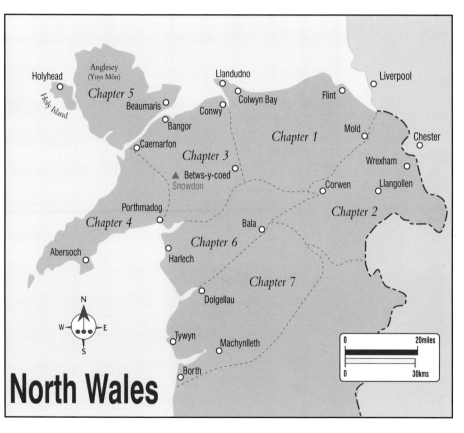

North Wales

Penrhyn Castle (National Trust)

Contents

Contents

Useful Welsh Words & Phrases

English–Welsh

Wales . . . . Cymru (cumree)

Welsh . . . . Cymreig (cumreyg)

England . . . . Lloegr (hloygr)

Englishman . . . . Sais (sysse)

Good morning . . . . Bore da

(borreh da)

Good afternoon . . . Prynhawn da (pnaown da)

Good evening Noswaith dda (nosswythe dha)

Goodnight . . . . Nos da (nos da)

Hello . . . . .Helo (helo)

Hi!, How are you? . . . . .Sut mae?

(sit mye)

Welcome . . . . Croeso (croy-so)

Goodbye . . . . Hwyl (hooil)

Bye . . . . Hwyl (hooil)

Good luck. .Pob lwc

(pawb look)

Welsh–English

Aber . . . . river mouth

Adwy. . . . . .gap, pass

Afon . . . . river

Allt . . . . wooded hill or cliff

Aran . . . . high place, mountain

Bach .small, corner

Bala . . . . joining of lake to river

Banc . . . . .bank, hill

Bedd . . . . grave

Bont . . . . .bridge

Bron . . . . breast of hill or slope

Bryn . . . . .hill

Bwlch . . . . .head of the pass or col

Bychan . . . . small

Cadair . . . . seat, stronghold

Cae . . . . field

Caer . . . . .fort

Capel . . . . chapel

Carn . . . . .cairn

Carreg . . . . stone

Carrog . . . . .stream

Cefn . . . . .ridge

Celli . . . . grove

Clogwyn . . . . cliff, precipice

Clwyd . . . . .gate

Coed . . . . trees

Craig . . . . rock

Crib . . . . .ridge

Croes . . . . cross, crossroads	Mam . . . . .mother
Din, Dinas . . . . .fort	Mawr . . . . great, extensive
Dre . . . . homestead	Melin . . . . mill
Drws . . . . .door, pass	Merch (plural Merchedd) . . . .
Du, Ddu . . . . .black	. . . . .woman
Dwy . . . . .two	Moel . . . . bare or rounded mountain
Dyffryn . . . . valley	Morfa . . . . coastal marsh
Eglwys . . . . church	Mynydd . . . . .mountain
Erw . . . . acre	Nant .brook, valley
Esgair . . . . .long ridge	Neuadd . . . . hall
Fach . . . . small	Newydd . . . . .new
Fawr . . . . .large, great, extensive	Nos . . . . night
Fechan . . . . small	Ogof . . . . cave
Ffair . . . . .fair	Penrhyn . . . . headland
Fford . . . . road	Pant . . . . hollow ground
Ffraw . . . . .rapid	Parc . . . . field
Ffrith . . . . .meadow	Penmaen . . . . .rocky headland
Foel . . . . bare hill	Pennant . . . . head of valley
Fychan . . . . small	Pentre . . . . .village, hamlet
Garth . . . . .hill	Pig . . . . summit
Glan . . . . .brink, edge	Pistyll . . . . waterfall
Glas . . . . .blue, green	Plas . . . . hall
Glyder . . . . sheltered valley	Pont . . . . .bridge
Glyn . . . . valley	Porth . . . . harbour, bay
Gwydd . . . . trees	Rhos . . . . .moorland
Gwyddfa . . . . .wild place	Rhyd . . . . ford
Gwynt . . . . wind	Saeth . . . . arrow
Hafod .summer home	Sarn . . . . .causeway
Hen . . . . old	Tal . . . . .front
Hendre . . . . winter home	Tan . . . . below
Hyll . . . . .ugly	Traeth . . . . .beach
Isaf . . . . .lower	Tyn . . . . .small farm
Llain . . . . stretch of land	Tywyn . . . . shore
Llan . . . . .church or enclosed space	Uchaf . . . . upper
Llanerch . . . . .clearing glade	Wen . . . . white
Llech . . . . .stone slab	Y . . . . the
Llety . . . . .small house	Yr . . . . the
Llyn . . . . .lake	Ynys . . . . .island
Maen . . . . .stone	Ysbyty . . . . .hospital
Maes . . . . field	Ystryd . . . . street

Arriving in North Wales for the first time most visitors will be agreeably surprised by the change of scenery. From the border counties of England the hills rise gradually from the plains, getting more rugged and grander the further one journeys west. The border counties are green and luxuriant, the western counties craggy and steep and although the mountains are not as high as their counterparts in some European countries they are nevertheless equally impressive.

Top Tips

Visit:
- Caernarfon Castle
- Ffestiniog or Snowdon Railway
- The National Slate Museum

With Children:
- Welsh Mountain Zoo
- Rhyl Sun Centre
- Centre for Alternative Technology
- A child's excitment 'fishing' the rock pools of Shell Island

Views Not To Be Missed:
- Conwy Castle lit up after dark
- The mountains of Snowdonia from Beaumaris across the strait
- Mountains of Snowdon Horseshoe on a clear day

Many visitors will come solely to walk and climb in these hills, while many more will come for the glorious beaches that almost surround the region. Few parts of Great Britain are so accessible and can offer so much variety to the visitor; the combination of sea and mountains make it irresistible for many. One can be bathing on one of the many fine beaches and within the hour be heading for the summit of a mountain, though a change of dress would be recommended.

Recent years have seen a change in the pattern of holidaymaking throughout the country; no longer do we take our traditional two weeks beside the seaside but jet off to somewhere exotic for our annual holiday. When we stay in this country we tend to take shorter holidays or weekend breaks filled with activity or devoted to a special interest, walking, golfing, birdwatching to name but a few. North Wales fills this criteria perfectly, it is easily accessible has a reasonable climate and there are things to do all year round even in winter.

The larger coastal resorts offer excellent facilities for the tourist, good hotels, camping and caravan sites plus a range of activities for all ages. There has in recent years been an increase in visitor facilities besides the more traditional entertainments. You can go down a slate mine, make your own pottery, travel on a miniature railway, visit any number of museums, enjoy indoor water sports, outdoor water sports or visit a gaol. There are castles, ancient trackways to walk, and always beautiful scenery. There is something for everyone. There is never any need to be bored in Wales.

Many first time visitors to the region will naturally head for the better known areas. However, a little in depth investigation will uncover a vast amount of history, places and detail that can only enhance your visit. When you are visiting Wales (Cymru) you are also visiting a culture, a language and a heritage founded by the Celts more than 2000 years ago. The Welsh people are naturally warm hearted and honest but they do expect these feelings to be reciprocated. The Welsh language should cause the visitor few problems as all who do speak Welsh also speak English. You will see Welsh on signs and official documents; in theory since the Welsh Language Act of 1993 it has equal status to English. Road signs are now mainly in the Welsh form and businesses are taking pride in their language and many shop fronts now use it. Welsh names are used where possible throughout this book, while the Ordnance Survey has been used as the mediator if any doubt has arisen.

For the purposes of this book North Wales is taken to be the northern counties of Flintshire, Denbighshire and Gwynedd. Flintshire is that part of the north-east along the estuary of the Dee and adjoining the English counties of Cheshire and Shropshire; to the west is Denbighshire with its northern coast and the area of Conwy as its boundary. These two counties have about 50 per cent of the population of the whole of the area and certainly most of the industry around Wrexham (Wrecsam) and along Deeside. It also contains the larger coastal resorts of Rhyl, Colwyn Bay and Llandudno. They have their fair share of hills, castles and beauty spots. Close to the major cities of Liverpool and Manchester it is popular with day trippers. Clwyd was the old name for these northern counties but since 1992 they have reverted back to the old county names of Flintshire, Denbighshire and the newer Conwy and Wrexham. We have tried to be as accurate as possible within these fairly recent changes but the boundaries of each do not seem to be simple.

To the west and bordering the Irish Sea is the county of Gwynedd, with its beautiful coastline, its rugged mountains and quieter resorts. The two areas are as different as chalk and cheese. The shared county boundary is almost like crossing another border, for Gwynedd has a far greater proportion of Welsh speakers and one always feels closer to Wales in Gwynedd. Gwynedd also has the Snowdonia National Park as its heartland, with much of the finest scenery and the highest mountains in Wales and England.

The island of Anglesey, or Ynys Môn, separated by the narrow straits from the north-west coast, gives this varied county a further dimension. Gwynedd is considered by many to be the heart of Wales, epitomising every aspect of the country and its culture.

Snowdonia is the name that for centuries has been given by travellers to the mountains in the old county of Caernarfonshire. In 1951 these, along with the ranges of mountains to the south and the east were designated a National Park and the name Snowdonia was adopted as the official title of the park. As a park it extends from Conwy in the north to Aberdyfi in the south and from Bala in the east to Tremadog

in the west, roughly 50 miles (80.5 km) long and 35 miles (56 km) wide, though this does vary. Besides the mountains there are a multitude of lakes and 22 miles (35km) of coast are included with some of the finest beaches in Wales.

The National Park has fourteen peaks over 3,000 ft (914 m) with many more falling only a few feet short. The area is scantily populated by comparison with the adjacent counties and is almost purely Welsh speaking. It could be said that the sheep outnumber the people, and, even the sheepdogs only respond to commands given in Welsh.

Unlike National Parks in other parts of the world, Snowdonia and the other parks in Great Britain are all working areas. The people own the land, they work it and in most cases live on it. The balance between access for the visitor to any area within the park is generally with the goodwill of the owner and care must always be taken to leave the area as you found it, so take nothing but memories and photographs.

You will find many beautiful areas in North Wales. If you enjoy peace and tranquility you can easily escape from the hustle and bustle of modern life. There are quiet little valleys, beaches and villages. The area is so compact it is not difficult to enjoy a varied holiday without travelling too far.

The area considered in this book has been divided into sub areas and each has a separate chapter. There are suggestions for places to visit, things to do and walks to enjoy. These are unlikely to be the only attractions available and a little individual exploration will uncover a wealth of hidden pleasures.

There are few, if any, properties

Tan y Bwlch station, Ffestiniog Railway

Nant Peris from Pen y Pass at sunset

(either National Trust or privately owned) that are open all year round. It is always sensible to check visiting hours beforehand with the local Tourist Information offices.

Some walks are suggested, and while most are fairly easy and can be tackled by the average person, many – particularly within Snowdonia – are more arduous and should not be attempted without due preparation. As the weather can change quickly, extra clothing and waterproofs should always be taken on a long walk. A map, too, adds so much to the enjoyment. A 1:50,000 Ordnance Survey map of the area will be invaluable

Cromlech above Rowen on ancient road to Penmaenmawr

(Explorer Series 2.5 ins to 1 mile - 4cm to 1km). The maps ahow access areas. Many small areas and forests have their own nature trails or forest trails; individual leaflets are generally available at nearby information offices or shops.

Throughout this guide are suggestions for visits and walks, and at the end of the book is useful information for visitors. Every effort has been made to ensure the accuracy of the information and, though lack of space precludes much that may be of interest, it is hoped that visitors will use it as a basis for an enjoyable holiday.

History

Wales is a complex country with some of the finest scenery in the British Isles, three National Parks and a beautiful coastline to rival any in Europe. With its own language and culture and a great feeling for its roots, history and the influence of the landscape is never very far away. These are probably the major influences that have created the nation that we know today. The North Wales area has the highest mountains, some of the finest castles and much more a feel of real Wales than its southern counterpart, so a little background knowledge can only enhance your exploration and holiday.

Ancient history

Man's first forays were probably to the coastlands where he could survive on a diet of fish supplemented by the occasional wild ox or deer he could catch.

The burial chamber at Capel Garmon

His camps were temporary and we know little of his lifestyle; some caves he occupied close to Prestatyn which have been excavated, suggest that he was itinerant and show evidence that he may have been around just after the last Ice Age, approximately 18,000 years ago.

The first real evidence of man's in-dustry in North Wales are the stone axe 'factories' as at Craig Llwyd above Pen-maenmawr and Mynydd Rhiw on the Lleyn Peninsula. Examples of stone axes from here have been found throughout Great Britain, but whether they were traded, exchanged or bartered we will never know. They were certainly valued, perhaps they were the first souvenirs taken home by Paleolithic visitors to the country.

The land was mainly forests of pine and birch and what scant evidence is available from the stone age periods shows that early man preferred coastal sites, river banks or lakeside locations. Stone tools are occasionally found on these low lying areas.

Later visitors brought more advanced tools and domestic farm animals but it was not until the Bronze Age that any great impact was felt in the area. It was during this period that many of the surviving standing stones, hut circles and burial chambers were erected.

From around 1800 BC to 500 BC the Bronze Age people worked and traded in the area. However, they were gradually over-run by, or became intermingled with, a group of settlers from Europe bringing with them the techniques of iron working. These im-migrants were followed, in about 300 BC, by the first Celts who arrived from Gaul and settled mainly in the western areas of the country. Besides bringing agricultural skills they are noteworthy for the many hill forts they built in Wales, Tre'r Ceiri on Yr Eifl being a fine example.

It is likely that the roots of Welsh culture and probably the language lay with this pre-Roman group of settlers, though it is difficult to pin down with complete certainty. Celtic undoubt-edly formed the basis of the language used in many western areas of Britain and France around that time. There is a similarity with Gaelic in Scotland and Ireland and the Breton language in France.

Arrival of the Romans

The coming of the Romans in AD 43 further pushed the Celts to the peninsu-las and western areas of Britain, cutting them off even further from mainland influences. By AD 78 the Romans had conquered North Wales, though whether they ever subjugated the natives is doubtful. They built several forts as at Deva (Chester), used as the base for sorties into the hostile country. Segontium (Caernarfon) was the major base within Gwynedd with many smaller camps throughout the country. Many of the present roads follow the lines of early Roman roads. It is likely that the Roman influence was small and much of the activity was to maintain a presence and trade with the natives. There is evidence that during their oc-cupation the Romans mined gold and copper and other minerals, particularly lead, in the eastern areas of Wales.

In the fourth century AD the Romans

returned home to save their falling Empire and left the Celts to return to their former primitive life. They have, however, left some signs of their presence and though their forts were small they are fairly plentiful.

The Dark Ages

The next major influence came in the fifth and sixth centuries with the arrival of the first Christians from the Continent and Ireland. These priests and monks came to form the backbone of the Celtic Church and established many of the early churches, such as at St Asaph and Bangor. There was a post-Roman Christian movement and by the sixth century AD Celts had been converted from paganism to this new religion. The word was spread by itinerant saints who travelled the country creating religious settlements and building churches. The inclusion of 'Llan' coupled with the saint's name usually indicates such a place, such as Llanbadrig, The Church of Patrick, or Llandudno, The Church of St Tudno. Wales by the seventh century was fully converted and a major religious influence on the rest of the British Isles. There are many sites associated with those early wandering saints as at St Seriol's Well close to Penmon Priory on Anglesey and St Beuno's Well (Ffynnon Beuno) at Clynnog on the Lleyn Peninsula.

Medieval times

The Norman invasion of England in 1066 was followed by the gradual conquest of Wales, though the principality of Gwynedd in the north formed an almost impregnable bastion of high hills and mountains. It was Edward I in the thirteenth century who systematically built a ring of steel in the form of castles at Flint, Rhudlan, Conwy, Beaumaris, Caernarfon and Harlech, all of which could be supplied by sea and all were virtually impregnable on the landward side. Edward strengthened some of the Welsh princes' castles at Criccieth and Dolwyddelan and was not only able to control the coastlands but also the very heartland of the country. It was Edward who anglicised the organisation of the country and named his eldest son the first Prince of Wales.

The native Welsh princes from then on fought a spasmodic rearguard action culminating with the abortive Owain Glyndwr revolt in the fifteenth century. There is a cave above Beddgelert on the slopes of Moel Hebog romantically associated with Glyndwr, which is said to be his hideaway during his escape. This was the last serious attempt to overthrow the English crown and subsequent to this the Welsh influence was purely cultural, with the language playing a major unifying role throughout the country. The first Act of Union in 1536 virtually sealed the fate of the Welsh as a separate nation. They became beholden to English laws and in much of the land to English landlords; theoretically a Welshman was not allowed to own land without special permission. It was not until 1955 that Wales once more had its own capital city, Cardiff and in 1999 when it had an Assembly re-instated that it has now a large measure of Welsh affairs.

Aberglaslyn Pass, south of Beddgelert

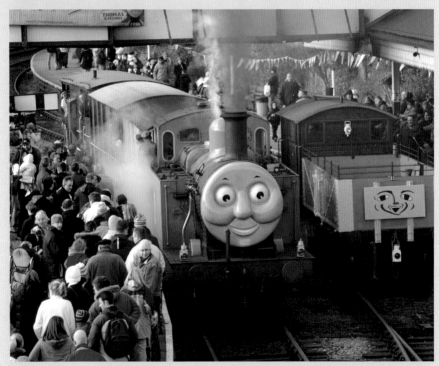

Thomas The Tank Engine attraction, Llangollen Station

Snowdonia from Beaumaris

Snowdon from near Rhyd-Ddu

The old slate mill at Cwmystradllyn

Industrial Revolution

The seventeenth century saw the industrial revolution arrive in North Wales with the mining of coal and iron around Wrexham, the mining of lead ore in the limestone hills in the north-east and copper in the mountains of Snowdonia. As you travel around you will see the great heaps of waste from some long dead mining operation, and there are few hillsides untouched by man's eager searches for profit.

Gwynedd is particularly rich in industrial archaeology; everywhere are the massive tips of the slate quarries and mines. North Wales is said to have roofed the world, providing much of the slate for the tremendous building projects during the industrial revolution.

The quarries are everywhere in the mountains, often on a huge scale; the mines have vast inner chambers where men worked in treacherous conditions for a pittance. The scale of these burrow-ings are often difficult to believe, particularly now all is quiet and little evidence remains of those who worked them. Ports developed around the coast specifically to handle the products from these enterprises, and were served by tramways and railways direct from mine to quay. For instance on the Ffestiniog-Porthmadog route, populations grew around both ends of the line and gradually the communities took shape.

Modern times

They are the villages and townships which exist today, but though the streets and houses are the same, eco-nomic conditions have changed. The mines and ports are closed, alternative work has had to be found or created, and while in most cases this has been successful, conditions can still be hard in the hills. The communities are still there, though depleted, vacant houses have been sold for weekend cottages as tourism has become a major industry. The old railways have been revived to carry tourists, the old mines are now museums, the ports cater for yachts-men and fishermen, old crafts have been re-discovered and marketed, the hills are now being walked for leisure instead of necessity. The whole country has seen greater changes during the last 100 years than at any time during its previous history.

Today's visitor should take plenty of time to explore, and those who look deeper than the surface will find a wealth of interesting places to be discovered and so will enjoy their visit even more.

The Language

It is known with some certainty that the Celts who populated Britain from Europe in the fourth century BC brought not only their iron working skills but also their language. Those who arrived in Wales spoke Brythonic or a British language similar to that spoken in Brittany and Cornwall.

Pressures of the Roman invasion forced the Celtic people into the western areas of Britain where they became further isolated and the lan-guage began to develop on its own. In later centuries the subsequent invasion of the island by the Anglo-Saxons from Europe pushed the Celts into the extremities of the country, into Wales, Scotland and Cornwall.

During each occupation the developing language borrowed words freely from the invasion force and for much of the time they lived in peace. The language continued to adopt words from other visitors including Norman French through to medieval English and right up to modern English. Other languages developed in a similar fashion.

Welsh was the main spoken language in the principality until the seventeenth century. The English influence, however, was spreading, as wealthy traders found it more convenient to be bilingual. English was also becoming used more widely for state purposes and as a public medium.

The church continued to use Welsh and through recent centuries has been the saviour of the language. Bishop Morgan had translated the Bible into Welsh in 1588 and this alone had ensured the survival of the language more than any other single act.

Nowadays many Welsh people are bilingual, particularly in western areas of the country like Gwynedd, less so in the border counties and on the northern coastlands where English is their first and frequently their only language. The Welsh language is taught in most schools and all official documents must now be bilingual. Recent years have seen a swing to using the Welsh form on road signs and maps. There is now a widespread interest in the language and culture and though only a small proportion of the whole country is Welsh speaking, there is a revival in the customs and traditions of the country and much is being done to ensure the survival of the language.

The visitor to Wales will see place names that are different and will hear people speak in a very different language. This can be baffling to the non-Welsh speaker, while finding your way around can be a daunting task particularly if you have to ask your way.

Many place names are descriptive of the physical feature of the area, eg, Moelwyn Mawr means the big bare hill. Others are named after the local church; hence the predominance of the names preceded by Llan, church of, as in Llanbadrig which means the church of Patrick. It can add interest and enjoyment to any holiday to try to solve the mystery of the language and find out where you are. A few words that may be useful are given; most are found in place names.

The ancient bridge at Llanrwst

Flintshire, the most northern and probably the smallest of Welsh counties is a fine mixture of gentle limestone hills and the great range of the Clwydian hills stretching for 20 miles (32 km) south from Prestatyn. The coastal plain is a narrow belt squeezed between the hills and the sea, unfortunately much of it alongside the Dee estuary bearing the remnants of old industrialisation; however it is soon passed or can be avoided. The county as a whole is a nice blend of rural farmland, hills and some seaside.

Its neighbour to the west, separated by the great Vale of Clwyd is Denbighshire, fairly similar with many popular resorts along its coastal belt. Inland it is again rural farmland and a complex of small hills and narrow roads, though to the south of the county there is a lovely area of high moorlands and forest.

The lowlands alongside the sea have provided the main thoroughfares to northern Wales for thousands of years and with the coming of the railways

Opposite: Llandudno Bay from the Gt. Orme

Left: The Welsh Mountain Zoo, Colwyn Bay
(Photo Credit: Welsh Mountain Zoo)

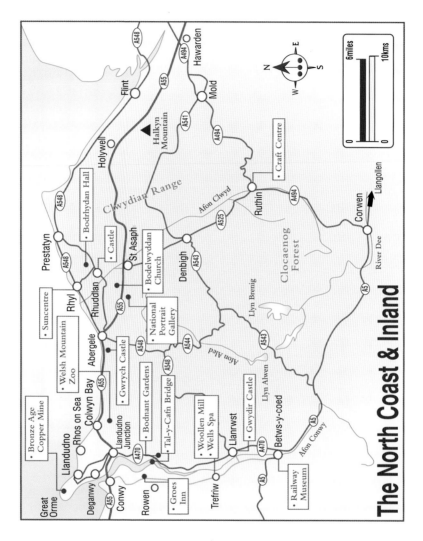

The North Coast & Inland

opened up a new form of relaxation for the working person, a day at the seaside, transforming the small Welsh villages along the coast of both Flintshire and Denbighshire into holiday centres.

A feature of both counties are the deep river valleys bisecting the hills and the access they provided through the ages for friend and foe. The road builders used them when they developed the modern road systems and they are in the main still the best way of moving around the country swiftly.

The River (Afon) Conwy is perhaps

one of the most famous rivers in Wales, so for the convenience of delineation it has been used with the county of Conwy as the western boundary of this area. There has in recent years been a substantial effort to increase the number of visitor activities in the area and there is now much to see and do with still time to relax on the beach afterwards.

The lands bordering the coast are generally low lying with a belt of hills behind them. There is a choice of roads from Queensferry, either the inland route, the A55 which is a fast dual carriageway, or the more scenic coastal road the A548, giving easy access to all the northern resorts. Nowadays with the wonderful new Flintshire Bridge crossing the Dee from Cheshire, Queensferry and the less scenic parts of Deeside can be avoided. On both routes there are many reminders of the area's turbulent history, particularly of Edward I's attempts to subdue the Welsh princes in the late thirteenth century, when he built castles at all strategic points to maintain law and order. There are many fine ruins from this 'ring of steel' for the visitor to enjoy, most of them only slightly off the beaten track.

The Dee Estuary

After crossing the River Dee at Queensferry or Chester the coastal road follows for several miles the culmination of hundreds of years of industrialisation. Though the estuary is never more than a mile away, it is only glimpsed occasionally between the mammoth buildings, many of which are now redundant. Fortunately this zone is limited to a very narrow belt, backing on to the estuary, and can be easily avoided by using the inland route or the bridge linking North Wales with the A550.

Inevitably, after conquering Wales, Edward I built a fortification on the first high ground after Chester. He chose the site of an Iron Age fort at **Hawarden** and there built a stone castle with a round tower. Some parts remain today, but much of it was destroyed in 1646. It is not open to the public.

Just two miles away from Edward's castle at Hawarden stand the remains of **Ewloe Castle**, now surrounded by trees and not visible from the road. It was built by Llewelyn the Last about 1260 and is typical of a Welsh stone

Gladstone's home

A later house, started in 1750 and still standing below the castle, was the home of one of Queen Victoria's Prime Ministers, William Gladstone, who acquired the estate when he married Catherine Glynne. He lived there for sixty years and the neat little village bears many reminders of this most famous resident particularly the fountain in the centre of the village, There is also a Gladstone museum, a commemorative window and an effigy in the church almost opposite the main gates to the estate, and a statue also near the gates. Next to the church in Hawarden is the *Deiniol Library* founded by Gladstone in 1895 and housing a collection of theological books and pamphlets which are available for study.

castle, built to provide a buffer between the warring English and Welsh. Rather strangely it is built on the side of a small valley and not in a prominent position as is usual; the castle and surrounding woodlands have now been incorporated in **The Wepre Country Park** which has an interpretation centre, good walks, swings and picnic tables. The main entrance is signposted from the A548 close to Queensferry.

It is difficult now to imagine the importance of this area in past times; it was the main route into Wales from Chester and England, for the hills further inland were inhospitable and dangerous to cross. The coastal belt was the main highway for all invading armies from the Romans onwards. As it is also easier to supply armies by sea than over land, the area has always been strategically important.

To complement the castle at Hawarden, which guarded the inland route, Edward I built a fortress at **Flint** to protect the coastal route and the estuary of the Afon Dee. The castle, built on rock on the very edge of the sands, is all that remains of a once walled town. It is just off the main square and missed by the many visitors who head each year for the beaches further along the coast. One tower is detached from the main body of the castle and is connected by a drawbridge; it is the only example of this in the country. The tower or donjon was to be the last line of defence. The castle was the scene of the betrayal of Richard II and was immortalised in Shakespeare's play, much of which is set there. Today the castle is almost surrounded by buildings, and the Dee continues to silt up. The port

that flourished until the last century no longer exists and today the town relies on modern industry for its survival.

The county town is **Mold**, just five miles to the south of Flint. Unlike its predecessor it occupies a position of no particular geographical or historical importance, though it is a very pleasant little town. There was a small Norman castle on Bailey Hill at one end of the High Street, and the church, which is fifteenth-century, has some fine stained glass windows, and friezes carved with animals.

Mold was the home in the nineteenth century of Daniel Owen, a novelist and short story writer, who wrote in the Welsh language about Welsh people. He was a tailor who spent most of his life in the town. There is now a small museum at the **Daniel Owen Centre** containing memorabilia of this fine author.

Each Saturday and Wednesday the main street in Mold is closed for the market, the stalls of which are set up on each side of the road. On the outskirts is the **Theatre Clwyd**, a centre for entertainment and arts. There are regular concerts, and the theatre has its own company.

On the opposite side of the town the A494 Ruthin road rises steeply to the Rainbow Inn, before dropping even more steeply down to the Loggerheads Inn at the bottom of a deeply wooded valley. There is a car park here and short walks can be taken along the valley and through the woods – a pleasant spot to spend an afternoon. There are some steep limestone cliffs above the woods which give a feeling of depth to this little valley.

Between Mold and Denbigh is the

Above: Ruddlan Castle

Opposite: Bodnant Gardens (N.T)

Below: Below: Ruddlan and the River Clwyd

village of Afonwen. It contains a craft centre with antiques, furniture, curios and collectables.

Continuing along the main Ruthin road a minor road, probably the original road, turns off to the right about one mile after Loggerheads. If one takes this to the top of the pass and parks for a short while there are some breathtaking views over Ruthin and the Vale of Clwyd to the north and the sea.

From the car park the single track road descends steeply into Ruthin and requires care.

To the north of Mold is **Halkyn Mountain** which runs nearly parallel with the estuary. It is composed mainly of limestone and for many centuries was the source of much of the wealth of the county; it was riddled with lead and lead mines. There are many remains of engine houses and tunnels of interest to the industrial archaeologist. The Romans mined here but it was the nineteenth-century entrepreneurs who used their technology to sink even deeper mines and longer tunnels. Water seepage was always a serious problem and it was not until 1878 that a tunnel (sough) almost the full length of the mountain drained the mines into the estuary.

Today the hill is extensively quarried for limestone, but for walkers there are excellent views across the Dee estuary, the Wirral and the Mersey estuary to Liverpool and the Lancashire plain.

On the northern slopes of Halkyn Mountain stands the small town of **Holywell**, once a centre for many pilgrims. Known as the Lourdes of Wales, the once natural well is said to have curative powers and is part of **St Winifride's Chapel**, a chapel built in about 1500 in the perpendicular style by Margaret Beaufort, the mother of Henry VII. Pilgrims enter the bath by steps or they can be carried through, and then kneel to pray on the stone of St Beuno, founder of an earlier chapel on the site. The Holy Well was originally fed by a spring from the nearby limestone hills, but since the early part of this century has been supplied by a small reservoir. The architecture for such a small building is magnificent. It is a lovely place though enigmatic and to an extent sorrowful. The well can be visited for a small contribution.

Until the Reformation, the well was in the care of the Cistercian monks from nearby **Basingwerk Abbey**. The abbey, just a short distance further down the valley to the north in a beautiful setting and built of sandstone of wonderful colours, was known for its fine building and windows. It was taken apart at the Dissolution and the present remains, which are mainly thirteenth-century (though the original abbey was founded in 1132), give some idea of the extent of the building. A park now surrounds the remains with access by a visitor centre.

Both St Winifride's Well and the Abbey are set in the **Greenfields Valley** which has historical connections with the lead mining on nearby Halkyn Mountain. There are now historical displays of the methods used in the whole of the lead industry, an interpretation centre and a farm museum. In recent years much time and effort has been spent on improving this area and making it a fascinating place to visit.

North-west of Holywell, near

Whitford, is **Maen Achwfan**, an impressive early eleventh-century stone cross elaborately carved with Celtic designs. Standing 11ft (3.4m) high it is the tallest of its type in Britain. It is signposted from the nearby village.

Many visitors in the summer will be content to bypass the towns backing the Dee Estuary and speed west along the coast to the seaside towns and caravan parks which for many are the attractions in this part of Wales. From the disused colliery at the Point of Ayr the fields bordering the coastal road become a continuous mass of caravan sites and holiday camps which from Easter onwards attract visitors from all over Britain. It is a popular area for family holidays and weekend visitors, as there are many fine beaches along this northern coast which are safe for bathing and boating.

Coastal Holiday Towns

Talacre is perhaps the first real holiday area to be encountered on this section of the coast; its collection of small bungalows and big caravan parks nestle snugly behind the sand dunes. Many years ago it was well known for its motley collection of 'chalets' built of wood, corrugated metal sheets or seemingly anything that was available; these are all gone and it is now a pleasant little resort. Close by is the **BHP Gas Terminal** which has a recently opened visitor centre with displays about its function and purpose.

Prestatyn, the first major town to be reached, has its town centre set well back from the beach almost as if it does not want to admit to being one and the same. At the time of writing this may be understandable. There are three main beaches, **Ffrith beach**, the most northerly, has convenient parking, a play area with motor boats, a mini-golf course and other amusements. **North Wales Indoor Bowling Centre** is here. This is not ten pin, it is a superb eight-rink indoor bowling green, built to international standards, with shoe and bowl hire available. It could be an ideal place to spend a wet day. Competition can get fairly serious but visitors are admitted to watch and to play.

Central beach has the **Nova Centre** backing onto it, a heated swimming pool if the sea is too cold, band concerts and bars. **Barkby beach** is perhaps a little quieter and has access for boat trailers. Central and Ffrith beaches are the best for bathing.

The town itself is a thriving community all the year round with many residents, and does not rely solely on

Fine views

From the parking spot there is a good footpath leading up to the Jubilee Tower on the summit of Moel Famau. The tower was built to commemorate George III's jubilee. It is now part of a country park and on a clear day one can sometimes see the Isle of Man and the mountains of the Lake District to the north; but the closer views of Snowdonia to the west are more rewarding. It is a pleasant stroll, well worth doing.

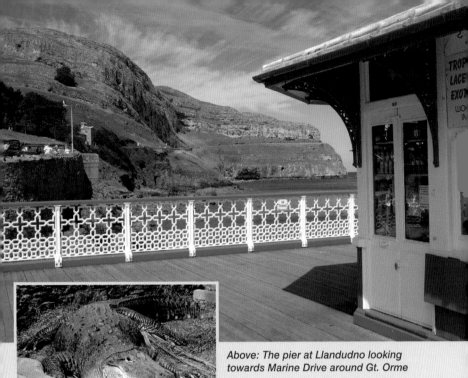

Above: The pier at Llandudno looking towards Marine Drive around Gt. Orme

Above: The Welsh Mountain Zoo, Colwyn Bay (Photo Credit: Welsh Mountain Zoo)

Right: The Punch and Judy show, Llandudno Promenade

St Winifride's Well

Legend tells us that it was at this spot in AD 606 that the head of young Winifrede fell after an enraged local chieftain severed it for spurning his advances. She was restored to life by her uncle St Bueno and the spring became famed for its healing powers. Pilgrims have travelled from all over the world for many centuries to seek its curative powers. Holywell has been a place of pilgrimage since the seventh century and is the only place in Britain with an unbroken history of pilgrimage from then until the present day.

Rhyl is only 4 miles (6.4km) from Prestatyn, but it seems much more on a busy Sunday when the traffic moves slowly. Perhaps the most famous seaside town in North Wales, catering for many thousands of visitors each year, it differs completely from its near neighbour and is so much more brash. There is something for everybody with all the necessary seaside amusements on the promenade, and a beach which is excellent for swimming, though one must take care at the western end near the mouth of the River Clwyd. Most of the major attractions are along the sea front on the wide promenade. **The Sun Centre** dominates the Eastern Parade, a large modern structure mainly of glass containing restaurants, amusements, a swimming pool with a wave-making machine and other swimming pools.

Greenfields Valley

Now a Heritage Park it fills the valley to the north of Holywell. The use of water was harnessed to power a series of reservoirs and mills manufacturing a variety of industrial and domestic items from the mid-eighteenth century onwards. These included copper and brass pans, rolled copper sheets, brass wire and even a cotton mill.

A footpath runs the length of the valley, following the old railway which at one time was the steepest in the country. There are displays, visitor centres and lots to see and investigate, including of course a Holy Well and a wonderful ruined Abbey.

summer visitors for its livelihood. There is a good range of shops, cafés and hotels. Inland from the coast is **Meliden**. Above Meliden is a range of limestone hills with several short walks which give excellent views all along the coast.

Above Prestatyn on the road out to Gwaenysgor, there is a small car park before the road climbs steeply; the signpost shows the route to **Offa's Dyke Path** and a walk through the woods up to the top of the hills. This is the northern end of the Offa's Dyke Path and for many walkers it is the culmination of a long walk up the borders of Wales. Crowning the hill are the embankments of an old Iron Age fort. Just to the south at **Gop Hill** are some caves where remains of Stone Age man have been found. For the archaeologist this area is particularly fascinating, for there is much evidence of prehistoric man.

Further along the Promenade close to the middle town is the **Sea Life Centre** and the **Children's Village**, a paddling pool and bandstand, and towards the very end is the **Ocean Beach Park** with its roundabouts and all-the-fun-of-the-fair.

The Sky Tower can be spotted from anywhere along this very pleasant promenade. Other amusements seem to come and go along the promenade, which unfortunately may reflect the change in pattern of the British holidaymaker. Walk along the promenade take in the sea air and experience the real Rhyl, it is a place for all the family.

The west promenade of Rhyl has undergone a transformation, seaside gardens with panoramic views of the coast. The new multi-million pound design, known as Drift Park, is inspired by shapes and forms of the tide. It boasts an open-air theatre, mini golf, play zone and interactive play area.

The estuary of the Clwyd effectively forms the end of Rhyl but just three miles to the south alongside the river is **Rhuddlan Castle** another, and perhaps the most solid looking, of Edward's castles so far. It was built at this major crossing point and the river was canalised to allow supply by ships from the sea. It stands as a grim reminder to the modern visitor of the troubled past of this land.

The White Marble church at Bodelwyddan is in fact limestone on the exterior but is perhaps one of the most beautiful churches in North Wales. It was built in 1856 and is dominated by its graceful tower 203ft (62m) high. It is visible for many miles. In the southern part of the cemetery are the graves of 23 Canadians who died at the nearby Kinmel Camp whilst waiting for repatriation after World War 1. The inside of the church is white marble and is unique; it is altogether an unusual building.

Close by is Bodelwyddan Castle home of the National Portrait Gallery, where a fine collection of scientists, politicians and Welsh notables hang in beautifully refurbished rooms. The house is set in extensive gardens and woodlands with nature trails, a playground and even some practice trenches remaining from the training of troops in World War 1.

The great beauty of the county is that everything is so accessible and always within easy reach of the seaside, it can cater for all ages and interests.

The coastal road continues parallel with the sea through the fields of caravans to **Abergele**, just 4 miles (6.4 km) further on. This small town seems to be more Welsh than its neighbour. At the junction of several main roads, its narrow streets are always busy. It is a market town and the old church close to the town centre contains some interesting relics of the past, with some fifteenth- and sixteenth-century glass and a dug-out chest. The churchyard has two memorials to disasters that happened in the neighbourhood, the shipwreck of the Ocean Monarch in 1848 and the crash of the Irish Mail train twenty years later.

Although situated about a mile from the seashore, Abergele, now joined to Pensarn on the coast, with its pebbly beaches and sandhills, is a pleasant town for a more relaxing day.

On the outskirts of the town are the long walls and great gatehouse surrounding **Gwrych Castle**, set below wooded hills in a large estate. It was an impressive site, though unfortunately a folly, for the castle was built in 1815 by a wealthy tycoon. It housed many antiques and fine furnishings but it has declined in recent years and is now approaching a state of near dereliction. There are several short walks in the parklands and surrounding woodlands.

In recent years the A55 has been upgraded and now speeds up and over the headland to **Penmaenrhos** with its huge limestone quarries, and then drops steeply down into the outskirts of Colwyn Bay.

Before the descent there is a fine viewpoint beside the main road where the sweep of the bay around to the Little Orme can be seen. The whole shoreline has beautiful sandy beaches with a promenade running almost the

Beaches & Entertainment in Prestatyn and Rhyl

Ffrith Beach
Prestatyn
Motor boats, children's play area, and other attractions.

North Wales Bowls
Ffrith Beach, Prestatyn
☎ 01745 886100
Motor boats, children's play area, and other attractions.

Central Beach
Prestatyn
☎ 01745 888021
Nora Centre, swimming pool.

Barkby Beach
Prestatyn
Good for launching boats, quieter than other beaches.

Rhyl Beach
Three miles of sandy beach, backed by a promenade. Cafés, children's playground, donkey rides, cinemas and all the fun of the fair. Punch & Judy shows

on selected dates. *Bathing is not advised on the western end near the mouth of the Afon Clwyd.*

Rhyl Tourist Information
☎ 01745 344515
rhyltic@denbighshire.gov.uk

Rhyl Miniature Railway
☎ 01352 759109

Sea Quarium
Promenade, Rhyl
☎ 01352 759109

Sun Centre
On Promenade, Rhyl
☎ 01745 344433
Super modern swimming pools, with wave-making machine, café etc, all in glass-sided building.

Ocean Beach Park and Marine Lake
West end of Promenade, Rhyl.
Swings and roundabouts and all the fun of the fair.

The Gt. Orme tram awaits
more passengers

The 'marble church' at Bodelwyddan, built in 1856

full curve of the bay.

Colwyn Bay, with its neighbour **Rhos-on-Sea**, has mushroomed in recent years to become a major holiday resort. Besides all the usual attractions along the promenade, including a pier, now sadly in need of attention, it has much to offer and many places of interest. **Eirias Park** runs south from the promenade, with picnic areas, boating, bowls, tennis and a sports area. The nearby **Prince of Wales Theatre** has a busy summer season with a variety of shows, while in Rhos there is the **Harlequin Puppet Theatre** just off the promenade and a golf course.

The bulk of the holiday traffic that used the main street to wind its way through the town has mainly been diverted to the A55. This seems to divide the long promenade and seashore from the town centre giving a slightly disjointed feeling to the area.

A curiosity on the seashore at Rhos is the miniature **church of St Trillo** built over a small holy well. The chapel is only 11ft by 8ft (3.4m x 2.4m) and is probably the smallest in Wales. The Celtic saint is believed to have lived here for many years and local people say fishermen and sailors prayed there before a journey. Services are now held outside, and the church is open daily.

On the outskirts of the town is the famous **Welsh Mountain Zoo** where a wide variety of birds and animals are kept in as near natural surroundings a possible. There are many birds of prey, and weather permitting, daily flying displays of eagles, falcons, etc. Behind Rhos on Sea is the small **Bryn Euryn**. Although almost surrounded by roads it is nevertheless a pleasant place to stroll

and to enjoy the panoramic views over the towns and the bay.

Llandudno and the Great Orme

The road climbs over the shoulder of the **Little Orme** and then descends to follow the promenade to **Llandudno**, sheltered on a neck of land by the massive bulk of the **Great Orme**. The town straddles the low-lying land with the main amusement centres on the north-facing coast and the quieter residential areas overlooking the estuary of the River (Afon) Conwy. The town retains much of its Victorian grandeur and gives the impression of being more conservative than its neighbours.

The promenade follows the curve of the bay, which is wide and airy leading on to a broad shingle beach. It is an elegant seafront with its Victorian hotels leading along to the pier at the foot of the Great Orme. The pier (longest in Wales) with its pavilion sits below the headland and seems to be almost in the centre of the town but perhaps one of the best outings is to drive past the entrance and follow the **Marine Drive** right around the Great Orme. The views out to sea and of the coast are fantastic.

The North Shore is dominated by the **North Wales Conference Centre and Theatre** but just behind and parallel are the main shopping streets, many shops still with their elegant canopies across the pavements. Near the pier is **Happy Valley**, a public park where everybody should be made to smile; it has playgrounds, rock pools and a ski

Food & Drink

With Conwy mussels, prime Welsh Black beef and Saltmarsh lamb, North Wales has a solid platform for its local produce. Locally landed seabass and lobster is available and the Conwy Honey Fair in September is a mecca for discerning honey lovers. The Conwy Brewery even produces a honey beer alongside its more traditional good quality beers. The sea yields other food too, with Pacific rock oysters grown commercially in the Menai Strait in competition with the mussell crop further along the coast. Amongst the best of local produce, look out for Anglesey seasalt (Halen Mon) and Welsh herbs from CaeGwyn Herb Nursery, also on Anglesey ☎ 01248 470231. Over at Holt, Vernon's Butchers have won many national awards for the quality of their meat and Edwards's in the High Street, Conwy have a high reputation too. It is recommended to lookout for other small local breweries including Gt. Orme Brewery.

Food Festivals

March
Conwy Seed Fair ☎ 01492 650851

August
Eglwysbach Agricultural & Horticultural Show ☎ 01492 650529
Llanwrst Agricultural Show ☎ 01492 650847

September
Conwy Honey Fair, High Street ☎ 01492 650851
Mold Food & Drink Festival

October
Llangollen Food Festival ☎ 01824 705802
Erddig Hall Apple Festival ☎ 01978 355314
Gwledd Conwy Feast ☎ 01492 593874

November
Llandudno: Celtic Winter Fayre. Over 100 food & craft stalls.
☎ 01492 574504

Farmers' Markets
See page 181

and activity centre. From the park a cabin lift leaves for the summit of the Great Orme.

On the other side of the town, the West Shore, overlooking the Conwy estuary and Snowdonia, it is generally quieter. It was here that Charles Dodgson, better known as Lewis Carroll, spent several holidays at the house of Dean Liddell, whose daughter inspired the tales of Alice in Wonderland. A memorial portraying the White Rabbit from those tales was unveiled there in 1933 by Lloyd George. Sadly damaged by vandalism it was moved to West Shore.

The Great Orme dominates Llandudno and protects it from the prevailing westerly winds. A toll road (Marine Drive) encircles the headland, giving some fine views of the cliffs, caves and coast to the south. It is possible to reach the summit café (679ft [207m]) by car, foot, tramway or cabin lift. The latter two are a continuous daily service during the summer months. There are many minor antiquities on the hillsides and the **Great Orme Nature Trail** which starts in the Happy Valley is perhaps the best way to see them. It is also an excellent way of escaping from the hustle and bustle for a few hours and enjoying this magnificent setting; it is well worth exploring.

Birth of Llandudno

In 1849 a Liverpool surveyor met with the land agent of Lord Mostyn and proposed the building of a seaside resort on the marshy land below the Great Orme. The buildings were to be of a classical elegance and laid out in a grid pattern to reflect the curve of the bay.

The houses had to be raised above the marshland so tons of quarry waste were used; the workers cottages and the stables were consigned to the rear of the town and the back streets to avoid spoiling the beautiful buildings. The new town was accessible by train and a pier was built with facilities for a ferry from Liverpool. The town still retains much of its Victorian opulence; the streets are wide, the buildings grand but still with much of their original charm.

South of Llandudno

A short distance to the south of Llandudno and standing on the shores of the Conwy estuary is **Deganwy**. With its castle, now only a ruin, it has for many centuries guarded the northern entrance to the Afon Conwy. Today, with a sheltered harbour, it is a popular resort and centre for sailing.

One of the best known attractions in this area is **Bodnant Gardens**, the home of Lord Aberconway, five miles to the south of Deganwy. It is one of the finest gardens in Britain, well known for its wonderful collection of trees from all over the world. There are 80 acres of formal and informal gardens on the hillside overlooking the mountains of Snow-donia. In the spring there are magnificent displays of rhododendrons, azaleas, magnolias, camelias and a laburnum tunnel, which is spectacular when it is in full flower. In the summer there are formal rose gardens and herbaceous borders.

The house here is not open to the public. The garden is laid in terraces down the side of the valley. Below the lawns surrounding the house is a large pond surrounded by mature trees and

Tu-hwnt-i'r-bont tearoom

Suspension Bridge, Betwys-y-coed

A warm day at Llanfair Talhaiarn, south of Abergele

The parish church and River Conwy at Llanrwst

paths which lead down to a canal pond which features on many photographs of the gardens. Adjacent to this is the large area of woodland with magnificent rhododendrons. Below the wood in the bottom of the valley stands the estate watermill which the late Lord Aberconwy also presented to the National Trust.

Up river from Bodnant, squeezed between the steep hills and the meandering river, is **Llanrwst**, a solid Welsh market town. It is a town little altered by tourism, that serves a wide community in the surrounding hills and forests. The River Conwy has many outstanding bridges, not least of which is the beautiful arched bridge here. Said to have been built by Inigo Jones in 1636, it was commissioned by the Wynn family who lived in Gwydir Castle on the opposite bank. There are other reminders of this wealthy family in the old church off the town square.

East from Llanrwst

To the east of Llanrwst in the area bordered in the south by the inevitable A5 and in the north by the coast is a vast area of un-commercialised Wales. The hills to the north are gently rounded, crossed by a zig-zag assortment of minor roads. There are lovely little villages and surprise views which for the car-bound visitor makes a pleasant interlude away from the bustling coastlands.

There are high moorlands with famous grouse shoots and hills that will give a good day's walking at a relatively low level. Much of the area has been afforested.

In the centre of this area and signposted from most directions is **Llyn Brenig**, a reservoir opened by the Prince of Wales in 1976. Surrounding the reservoir and easily accessible for visitors is an area of unspoilt country. There are nature reserves and picnic areas around the lake and sailing and fishing on it. The information centre will provide details of the nature and history trails. It is perhaps one of the best areas in the county to look at prehistory. There is much evidence of early man with hut circles, burial mounds and enclosures dating from the Stone Age to more recent times. It is an area well worth exploring and within easy reach of the coastal resorts and close to a car park.

To the east is the historic former county town of **Denbigh** (known in Welsh as Dinbych), built a short distance above the river. The castle, built by Henry de Lacy in 1282 for Edward I, to help maintain law and order in the region, changed hands frequently between the Welsh and the English. It was finally destroyed by the Roundheads in 1645 after an eleven-month siege. Charles I had taken refuge there after his defeat at Rowton Moor near Chester. It has a large and beautiful gatehouse and some interesting defensive ideas built in, though little now remains. Nearby are the walls of Leicester's church begun by the Earl of Leicester in 1579 to replace St Asaph's cathedral, but never completed. The remains of the town walls to the north of this ruin show how important Denbigh was in the past.

H M Stanley, the adventurer and the author of the remark 'Doctor Livingstone, I presume' was born in Denbigh, and Sir Hugh Myddleton, who constructed London's water supply in the reign of James I, lived close by at Gwaunynog. Thomas Edwards a famous and well loved bard, and the author known as Twm o'r Nant, is buried in the parish church one mile east of the town.

Downstream from Denbigh is the cathedral town of **St Asaph**. Though the cathedral is perhaps less famous nowadays than the nearby white 'marble' church at Bodelwyddan it gives the place the status of a city, the smallest (as is the cathedral) in Great Britain. **The cathedral** is a squat building on the site of a church founded in AD 560 by St Mungo, who was succeeded in AD 573 by St Asaph, from whom the town takes its name. There has been a cathedral here ever since, despite Edward I's attempts to build an alternative at Rhuddlan. The present, much restored, building contains many features that have survived from earlier centuries. The Chapter Museum contains a fine collection of early religious manuscripts and Bibles, but it is open only by request and never on Sundays.

The **White Marble church at Bodelwyddan** is in fact limestone on the exterior but is perhaps one of the most beautiful churches in North Wales. It was built in 1856 and is dominated by its graceful tower 203 ft (62 m) high. It is visible for many miles. In the southern part of the cemetery are the graves of 23 Canadians who died at the nearby Kinmel Camp whilst waiting for repatriation after World War I. The inside of the church is white marble and is unique; it is altogether an unusual building.

Close by is **Bodelwyddan Castle** home of the **National Portrait Gallery**, where a fine collection of scientists, politicians and Welsh notables hang in beautifully re-furbished rooms. The house is set in extensive gardens and woodlands with nature trails, a playground and even some practice trenches remaining from the training of troops in World War I.

The great beauty of the county is that everything is so accessible and always within easy reach of the seaside, it can cater for all ages and interests.

Denbigh Town Wall

Above: Denbigh Castle

*Above & right:
Bodelwyddan Castle,
home of the National
Portrait Gallery*

Places to Visit & Activities

Harwarden

Daniel Owen Centre   W

Earl Road, Mold
Exhibition centre of local arts and
memorial museum to Daniel Owen,
one of Wales' leading novelists.

Ewloe Castle

Welsh castle built by Llewelyn the
Last, to keep watch on Hawarden
Castle. Two miles (3.2 km) from
Hawarden on A55.

St Demiol's Library   W

Hawarden
A residential library containing
250,000 books.

Theatr Clwyd   W

Three theatres under one roof, regular
programme of films, concerts and live
exhibitions. Has its own professional
company. Close to town centre.

Holywell

St Winifride's Chapel

☎ 01352 713054
Built by Margaret Beaufort, mother of
Henry VII, it houses the Holy Well. A
destination for pilgrims for centuries.

Basingwerk Abbey

Off A548, 1 mile (1.6 km) north of
Holywell
☎ 029 2082 6185
Praised for its beauty and setting.
Ruins fairly extensive. Free

Holywell Leisure Centre

☎ 01352 712027

Flint Castle (Cadw)

Castle Street
On edge of estuary with interesting
defensive features including separate
donjon. Off main square in town. Free

Abergele & Colwyn Bay

Abergele Beach

Pensarn
Pebble beach but sand exposed
as the tide recedes. Popular for
caravans.

Bodelwyddan Castle   W

National Portrait Gallery
Bodelwyddan, Rhyl LL18 5YA
☎ 01745 584060

Colwyn Bay Beach

A long curving beach, round the bay.
Good sand and safe bathing, very
popular.

Eirias Park

Colwyn Bay
Boating, bowls, tennis, picnic spots.

Prince of Wales Theatre   W

Abergele Rd, Colwyn Bay LL29 7RU
☎ 01492 532668
Regular shows, bands and plays.

Rhos-on-Sea

Extension of Colwyn Bay, with
Harlequin Puppet Theatre, and St
Trillo's church on the beach.

Places to Visit & Activities

Welsh Mountain Zoo

Colwyn Bay LL28 5UY
☎ 01492 532938
Collection of animals and birds of prey with free flying displays daily (weather permitting). Off A55 by West End Shopping Centre.

In & Around Llandudno

Beaches

North Shore: Good beach backed by promenade. Safe bathing, launch facilities and water skiing.
West Shore: Shingle, sea goes out a long way at low tide, so bathing is only when tide is in. Both Beaches have blue flag awards.

Bodnant Gardens (NT)

Tal-y-Cafn LL28 5RE
☎ 01492 650460
Beautiful gardens and woodlands, some of the finest in Europe. Especially noted for its rhododendrons in the spring. Six miles south of Llandudno Junction off A470.

Bronze Age Copper Mines   W

Gt. Orme LL30 2XG
☎ 01492 870447

Great Orme

Nature trails, tramway and cabin lift to summit. Dry ski slope.

Happy Valley

Park with playground, rock gardens and Dry-ski slope.

Lewis Carroll Memorial

West shore

Pier

☎ 01492 872818
With theatre and landing stage.

Rapallo House   W

Ffan Bach Road
Museum and arts centre with exhibits of local and national interest.

Alice in Wonderland Centre

3-4 Trinity Square
☎ 01492 860082

Bodafon Farm Park

Promenade LL30 3BB
☎ 01492 549060

Great Orme Country Park

☎ 01492 874151

Great Orme Tramway   W

Church Walks LL30 1AZ
☎ 01492 879306

Llandudno Sailing Club

Irving Road LL30 1BB
☎ 01492 549900

Llandudno Superbowl   W

Champneys Retail Park
☎ 01492 871349

North Wales Golf Club

Bryniau Road LL30 2DZ
☎ 01492 876878

Snowdonia Cycle Hire

34 Tan y Bryn Road LL30 1UU
☎ 01492 878771

Venue Cymru   W

North Wales Theatre, Promenade
☎ 01492 872000

Vale of Clwyd and Llanrwst

Bodelwyddan   W

Near St Asaph. White 'marble'
church, built in 1856. At side of A55

Denbigh Castle and Leicester's Church (Cadw)

Interesting remains of important
castle.

Gwydir Castle

Llanrwst LL26 0PN
☎ 01492 641687
Historic Tudor mansion, grounds
with peacocks. Across the river from
Llanrwst on B5106.

Gwydyr Forest

Extensive forests on west bank of
river with many walks and nature
trails. Leaflets available from
Forestry Commission, Gwydyr
Uchaf, Llanrwst.

Llyn Brenig

6.5 miles (10.5 km) from Denbigh off
B4501. LL21 9TT
☎ 01490 420463
Reservoir for sailing, angling, pony

trekking, has archaeological trail
and visitors' centre.

Rhuddlan Castle (Cadw)

Solid looking castle on the edge
of the Afon Clwyd. Historically
important, but much damaged as
source of local building materials.

St Asaph Cathedral   W

One of the early churches of Wales,
and smallest cathedral in Britain.

Trefriw Wells Spa   W

☎ 01492 640057
Conwy Road, Trefriw LL27 0JS
Spa products, tea room, open daily,
times vary.

Trefriw Woollen Mill   W

Main Road, Trefriw LL227 0NQ
☎ 01492 640462
Open: daily 9.30am-5.30pm, Winter
10am-5pm. Closed Xmas/New Year
Bank Holidays.
Working woollen mill, showing
all stages of the manufacture of
tapestries and tweeds from raw wool.
Free

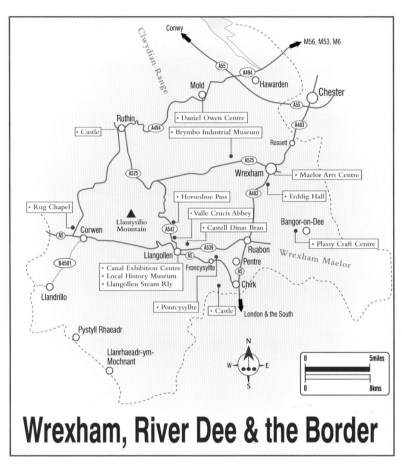

Wrexham, River Dee & the Border

Approaching Wales across the plains of Shropshire or Cheshire, the hills can be seen ahead for many miles. They sit dark and sombre along the horizon then almost immediately you cross the border you are amongst them, either climbing steeply or winding along deep valleys. The contrast between the landscapes of England and Wales is sometimes surprising and it is along these hills that Offa built his great dyke.

The Clwydian hills, stretching from the northern coast down to Llangollen and with the Berwyns to the south, form a natural boundary which in years gone by must have been formidable for travellers and invaders. They are in general comfortable hills, pleasing to the eye and pleasant, on a fine day, to stroll amongst.

Deeside

The **River Dee**, one of the major rivers of Wales, bisects these great ranges and winds through Llangollen, round far to the east of Wrexham and through the old city of Chester, Deva to the Romans, finally emerging to the sea at Flint to form the northern seaboard. There are few visitors to North Wales who will not cross it somewhere on their journey.

The eastern foothills which follow the curve of the Dee are composed mainly of coal measures with an underlying bed of limestone that comes to the surface occasionally as the scarp edges south of Maeshafn and on the Eglwyseg Mountains above Llangollen. It was probably the limestone deposits and the minerals in these hills, particularly lead ores, which brought the first industry to the area.

It is known that the Romans mined lead here using native labour, but it was not until the sixteenth and seventeenth centuries, when lead became such an vital commodity, that the industry really developed. The most important use for lead was the lining of the roofs of houses and churches. During the heyday of the lead industry money was invested heavily in mining in these limestone hills. The mines stretch from Halkyn Mountain (mentioned in previous chapter) near Prestatyn in the north to **Minera** west of Wrexham. Massive beam engines were brought up from Cornwall to pump the mines clear of water, but it is only the overgrown, square stone remains of the engine houses and their chimneys with the surrounding waste tips which survive as reminders of a once-thriving industry.

Minera lead mines

These have been active from medieval times until the mid 1900s. Much of the site has now been excavated and some working machinery installed. A Visitor Centre outlines the history of area and the site. Signposted from the Wrexham to Ruthin road, the A525.

Iron ore mined in the hills and coalfields surrounding Wrexham led to the establishment in the eighteenth century of a thriving smelting industry with iron works in Bersham, Ruabon and Wrexham. Other local resources, including clay for bricks and tiles, zinc ores, and wool from the local sheep, soon made this area the most industrialised and populous in North Wales. Bersham was the main supplier of cannons to the British army during the Peninsular War. The iron ore eventually ran out and the Wrexham-based industry was moved north to a site near Queensferry on the River Dee to allow direct imports of the raw materials by sea. During 1980, however, under Government rationalisation plans for the steel industry, this major employer on Deeside finally closed its doors.

Wrexham

Wrexham (Wrecsam) and its environs now support a few industries, but most of those based on local resources have declined, leaving their remains for the industrial archaeologist to explore. This area of Wales is now designated as a development area by the government, and industries large and small are encouraged to move here to provide much-needed employment.

In the centre of Wrexham stands the **church of St Giles**, notable for its decorated tower built in 1506 and surmounted by four graceful hexagonal turrets. To the west of the tower is the **grave of Elihu Yale**, the main benefactor of Yale University in America. It was restored by the members of the university in 1968 to mark the 250th anniversary of this benefaction. A replica of the tower of the church stands at Yale.

Around Wrexham

Virtually on the outskirts of Wrexham is **Bersham**, where John Wilkinson the famous eighteenth-century ironmaster worked. The cannon boring mill and remains of the furnaces still survive. They are the second oldest coke-fired iron furnaces in the world.

To the east of Wrexham is an area known as **Wrexham Maelor**, which projects into the plains of Cheshire and Shropshire. The district was originally known as Maelor Saesneg (Saxon Maelor) and was established by Edward I as a detached part of Flint. Its character is more English than Welsh, as are many of the village names, but it has firmly remained part of Wales through the

centuries, despite its vulnerable position. It finally lost its identity, and became part of Wrexham around 1995.

An important crossing point for the River Dee in this area was at **Bangor-on-Dee** (Bangor-is-y-coed), with its attractive old stone bridge, said to have been designed by Inigo Jones, and church. This small village was the site of the first monastery founded on British soil about AD 180. The monastery was destroyed in AD 607 by Ethelfrid of Northumbria, when 1,200 monks were slain. The few survivors are said to have established the first religious community on Bardsey Island. The main Wrexham to Whitchurch road now bypasses the village.

Bersham Heritage Centre and Iron Works

This dates from the seventeenth century and was one of the early leaders in the industrial revolution. In the eighteenth century John Wilkinson produced cannon for the great wars of the time, cylinders for James Watts' steam engine and worked closely with Telford on many of his great North Wales projects. There are exhibitions of industrial history of the area and the valley. Follow signs from A483 and A525 to Bersham.

About 1 mile (1.6 km) south of Wrexham and standing in a large estate, is the mansion of **Erddig Hall**, which was started in 1684 and finally completed about 1721–4 by John Meller, a London lawyer. With his nephew

Rossett Mill built in c.1474. Across the road from here is Marford Mill, with two more waterwheels

Simon Yorke he collected much of the fine silver and gilt furniture that can be seen here today. The property passed to Simon in 1733 and remained in the Yorke family until given to the National Trust in 1973. The family had always been good to their staff and the servants' hall has many portraits of particularly favourite staff. Visitors now enter through the stables and laundry, which, along with the restored sawmill, smithy and bakehouse, give a good idea of the domestic arrangements of an eighteenth-century house. There is a formal walled garden with old varieties of fruit trees, a dovecote complete with doves, extensive woods and parkland and a visitor centre.

On to Llangollen

Despite being the most industrial and extensively populated area of North Wales this corner of Clwyd has remained only a narrow strip. The nearby countryside is always accessible and only a short journey is necessary to leave all behind and reach the hills and valleys around **Llangollen**.

Here is a town so typically Welsh from its grey stone houses to its wooded hillsides that it is hard to believe that one is only a few miles from the English border. One needs go no further than Llangollen to experience much of what Wales has to offer, and it has justifiably been a popular tourist centre for many years. George Borrow started his epic Welsh journey here in 1854 by describing Llangollen in his book Wild Wales as 'a small town or large village'.

The town sits on both sides of the River Dee; the centre, with shops, cafés and hotels on the south bank of the river, is connected by a stone bridge to the thin strip of houses squeezed between the canal and the main road on the north of the river. The bridge was built originally in 1345, but it has been strengthened and improved through the centuries to cope with the increasing volume of traffic. This frequently causes quite a bottleneck on a sunny summer's day. Upstream of the town is a suspension bridge for pedestrians, known as the **Chain Bridge**.

The town is perhaps best known for the **International Musical**

Erddig, the garden front

Erddig from the Park

Eisteddfod which is held to the east of the town in July every year. It attracts singers, musicians and dancers from all over the world. The town comes alive with national costumes and a true spirit of international friendship during these weeks.

The International Eisteddfod in Llangollen started in 1947 as an annual meeting and competition of singers and dancers from all over the world. Every July it is a truly colourful spectacle as the town is so full of people from all nations in their own national dress.

Half a mile from the town centre is the old house of **Plas Newydd** (not to be confused with the National Trust house of the same name on Anglesey, overlooking the Menai Strait), once the house of two eccentric old ladies known throughout the country as the 'Ladies of Llangollen'. The ladies, the Hon. Miss Sarah Ponsonby and Lady Eleanor Butler, resided at the house from 1779 until their deaths in 1829 and 1831. They were known for their rather eccentric style of dress and for the variety of their visitors including Wellington, Sir Walter Scott, (who later immortalised the house in *The Betrothed*), and Wordsworth, all of whom were expected to contribute to the ladies' collection of old oak curios. Wordsworth's contribution was a rather disdainful sonnet, which was not liked by the ladies – he was not invited back.

Around Llangollen

There is not much room between the river and the steeply rising hills to the north, but in that short space is squeezed a railway station, now home of the Llangollen Railway Society, a busy main road and a canal. In this limited area it is possible to study transport through the ages, for just above the station is the **Canal Wharf Exhibition Centre** on a spur of the **Shropshire Union Canal**. This is appropriate as the Llangollen Branch was one of the earliest of Britain's derelict waterways to be restored for leisure cruising. Running from Hurleston Junction on the Shropshire Union Canal it passes through beautiful countryside on its way to Llan-gollen.

Climbing steeply from just opposite the canal bridge is a footpath to **Castell Dinas Bran**, a stone castle perched 1,000 ft (305 m) above the town.

Eisteddfod

These are unique to the Welsh culture, it means simply 'a session' and can be traced back to the twelfth century. At one time every village or town had an annual eisteddfod but over the centuries it has developed in to a place of serious competition amongst the Welsh Bards, musicians and dancers. There is one National Eisteddfod each year held in a different part of the country. The Gorsedd organizes the national competition for Welsh poetry that must follow clearly defined rules, the writer of the winning poem is crowned a bard and holds the chair for a year. It is a wonderful celebration of Welsh culture enjoyed by everyone.

Originally the site of an Iron Age hill-fort, it later became a Norman stronghold and, finally, a little-used stone castle built in 1236 which had become a ruin by 1578. The climber is rewarded by a fine view – the long limestone escarpment of **Eglwyseg Rocks** and the valleys radiating to the west and the north of the town. It is a magnificent place for a castle despite the fact it was of little significance.

A narrow road rises steeply from the bridge and runs up the valley below Eglwyseg Mountain to the ford at **World's End**. There is parking space below the ford and a short walk can be taken along the gorge onto the moorland and forests above. If you continue along the road it takes you out onto the open moorland, mainly sheep grazing land, before finally descending to the old lead mining community of Minera.

Fine aqueducts

The River Dee is at its wildest above Llangollen as it descends rapidly from just below the **Horseshoe Falls** in a series of small cataracts that tumble between the narrow banks – the venue of an annual canoe race. The Horseshoe Falls were built by Thomas Telford, the famous road and canal engineer, in 1806, to feed water into a spur of the Shropshire Union Canal running alongside and above the river before crossing 127 ft (39 m) above the river on the 1,000 ft (305 m)-long **Pontcysyllte Aqueduct** 3 miles (4.4 km) down river from Llangollen.

The aqueduct is a marvellous engineering achievement, as it carries the canal in an iron trough supported on eighteen tall, slim, stone pillars. The visitor with a head for heights can walk along the towpath across the aqueduct from either the canal basin at Trevor at the northern end, or park in a small car park at **Froncysyllte** at the other end and cross the canal by one of the waterway's characteristic lifting bridges. Perhaps the most impressive view of the aqueduct is not from the top, but from below. A recently improved path down to the River Dee starts from the Trevor canal basin and to look up at the stone pillars soaring above one's head makes it obvious why this was regarded almost as a miracle when it was first built, and as one of the wonders of the Industrial Revolution.

The Two Ladies of Llangollen

Lady Eleanor Butler and the Hon. Sarah Ponsonby, had a rather colourful history in their own right. Born and bred of Irish gentry they were not allowed by their families to cohabit so escaped across the sea to Wales setting up home in a small cottage on the outskirts of Llangollen in 1779 to 'devote their lives to friendship, celibacy and the knitting of blue stockings'. The eccentric lifestyle they shared together as they enlarged the cottage and devoted their lives to each other for 50 years, as well as their unusual style of dress made them famous throughout the land. The house is still a haven of the peace and tranquillity they must have enjoyed.

Chirk Castle and its garden

Wrexham Church, one of the wonders of Wales

Travellers from the south will miss Wrexham altogether and enter Wales close to the small border town of **Chirk**. To the west of the Telford A5 trunk road they will see an adjacent aqueduct and viaduct spanning the Ceiriog valley. The former carries the Shropshire Union Canal, and was built by Telford in 1801 and was the forerunner to the aqueduct across the Dee mentioned above. It was here he tried and tested his ideas before the much bigger undertaking of Pontcysyllte. The viaduct was built in 1848 to carry the railway and unfortunately took much of the goods of the so-recently built canal.

Unspoilt country

Chirk owes its origins to an eleventh-century castle built originally on the motte close to the church. This small Norman castle was superseded in the thirteenth century by a substantial stone castle built 2 miles (3.2 km) away by Edward I to protect the English/Welsh Border or 'Marches'. **Chirk Castle**, now owned by the National Trust, is the only Marcher castle to have been occupied continuously since it was built. For the visitor it has the contrast of a medieval castle with towers, courtyard, steep narrow stairs, bare cold guardrooms and a deep forbidding dungeon, with richly-appointed Adam-style staterooms. The beautiful formal gardens include notable topiary yew hedges and many flowering shrubs which are especially fine in springtime. A pair of magnificent wrought iron gates, made at Bersham in 1721, which once stood near the castle, now stand guard at the entrance to the 1.5-mile

(2.4 km) long drive.

The A5 trunk road, one of Telford's wonders, stretches from London to Holyhead and has been for more than a century and a half the main access to North Wales from England and the south. Running along the bottom of the Vale of Llangollen it provides many of the best views of the river and the surrounding hills. On the north side, the hills lean away from the road and are heather-clad in summer, but to the south the hills are heavily afforested and seem to become more so every year.

Rising steeply from the very back of Llangollen the road to Llanarmon Glyn Ceiriog and Llanarmon Dyffryn-Ceiriog takes one into some of the most beautiful countryside in North Wales. The narrow lanes meander steeply up and down the deep valleys as forests and hills vie for attention. Such a large area of Wales seems seldom to be visited and it has none of the trappings associated with tourism. It is crossed by only one road – fortunately an ancient trackway unusable by anything but four-wheel drive vehicles – but what a splendid route it is, going right over the ridge between Llanarmon Dyffryn-Ceiriog and Llandrillo, crossing the pass below **Cadair Bronwen**. The trackway itself is a wonderful walk giving easy access to the main Berwyn ridge and one can easily conjure up visions of invading armies struggling over in the cold and wet.

These hills, the **Berwyns**, provide some of the best walking for many miles and can be recommended for experienced walkers as one of the quietest and least frequented parts of North Wales, but one of the most easily accessible. The long ridge walk from **Moel Fferna** in the north, over the Berwyns to **Moel Sych** in the south is well worthwhile, but a map and compass will be essential and it is frequently wet underfoot.

Much of this countryside was explored by the intrepid George Borrow in the 1850s, as he walked many of the lanes and visited most of the villages. One of the towns he describes with little enthusiasm is **Llanrhaeadr-ym-Mochnant**, home of Bishop William Morgan who made the first translation of the Bible into Welsh during the reign of Elizabeth I.

Fine waterfall

Upstream from the village at the head of a steep sided valley is **Pistyll Rhaeadr**, the highest waterfall in Wales. Now largely surrounded by trees, it is difficult to appreciate the 240 ft (73 m) cascade from a distance. There is however a small car park by a quaint old farmhouse at the end of the lane and after a short walk one can see the full height from a bridge over the stream. The more intrepid walker can continue to the top of the falls by a steep footpath, starting from a grey gate opposite the farm, which zigzags up one side to the top, though this is a rather airy viewpoint. A walk upstream takes one into some fine country – the hills are wild, the ridge walks superb and the scenery splendid: but paths are rare, so go prepared.

To the west, the Berwyns drop slowly down to the Afon Dee as it casually meanders through the farming and forestry communities of **Llandrillo** and **Cynwyd**. Above Llandrillo on the

slopes of Cadair Bronwen is a prehistoric stone circle about 40 ft (12 m) in diameter. What its purpose and origin were we shall probably never know, but whoever placed it there chose the spot well, for the views of the hills and the valley and the feeling of spaciousness are outstanding. It was an ideal place for ritual meetings, if that was its purpose.

Joining the Afon Alwen, the River Dee turns east towards Llangollen, passing the market town of **Corwen** on its way. To the north the **Llantysilio Mountains** above Corwen are crowned by the Iron Age fort of **Caer Drewyn**. A few miles downstream between the road and the river is a small but significant mound which is almost certainly the site of the fortified manor of Owain Glyndwr the last Welsh Prince. Shortly beyond that at **Glyndyfrdwy**, named after the Glyndwr family estates, a delightful road wanders over the Dee and up into the hills. At its high point is a small parking area and an obvious path leading uphill to a lovely little summit with views along the hills and over the valleys. The heather-clad slopes run north-east to the top of the Horseshoe Pass, where the remains of the once thriving slate industry scar the landscape.

Near Corwen is Rug Chapel, built in the 17th century, with a lovely interior Tel: 01490 412025. A mile or south of Rug is Llangar Church of medieval age.

Thomas Telford

Thomas Telford crops up so often in this area a little background may be useful, though to be fair his name crops up throughout the British Isles – he was such a prolific engineer. He was the foremost engineer of his time becoming the founding father of Civil Engineering.

Born in Scotland in 1757 and apprenticed as a stone mason, he moved in his early twenties to London and developed his skills as an architect/ civil engineer, later becoming County Surveyor in Shropshire. He was given the task of linking the county with the developing network of canals in the country and particularly the ports of Merseyside. The Ellesmere Canal, later to become part of the Shropshire Union Canal, was the result and his very novel solutions to crossing the two deep valleys of the Ceiriog and the Dee remain to this day wonders of civil engineering. He was later awarded the contract to link London with the developing mail port to Ireland at Holyhead. This he did with the A5 trunk road, which to this day remains the main route into North Wales. Along this are some magnificent innovative bridges which we will cross later. Telford went on to design roads bridges and canals throughout the country. His energy and work was unbelievable and his scale of works both in design and construction has never been repeated. He died in 1834.

Llangollen

Valle Crucis Abbey

Horseshoe Pass

About 2 miles (3.2 km) to the north-east of Llangollen on the road to Ruthin before it crosses the Horseshoe Pass, is **Valle Crucis Abbey**, beautifully situated in the centre of what must have been an idyllic valley. The extensive ruins of the church and some of the domestic buildings, now almost surrounded by a caravan site, give an idea of the abbey's former size. It was founded by Madog ap Gruffyd in 1201 for the Cistercian Order, dissolved in 1535, and now stands to remind us of its former beauty.

The abbey is believed to have taken its name from the pillar standing about half a mile (0.8 km) to the north, **Eliseg's Pillar**, which stands on a mound. Originally a tall cross but now well worn, it was erected in the ninth century and was carved with a Latin inscription in memory of Eliseg who reclaimed Powys, an early Welsh kingdom, from the English in the eighth century. Perhaps Eliseg is buried under the mound.

The mountains are crossed here by the main Llangollen to Ruthin road by way of the famous **Horseshoe Pass**, where the road climbs around a huge cirque. It is justifiably popular and there is a viewpoint at the head of the pass looking down towards Valle Crucis Abbey and Llangollen. As the friendly sheep always seem to be hungry, car doors should be kept firmly closed. The Llantysilio Mountains, which the road crosses, continue eastwards to the **Eglwyseg Mountains**, which curve round to the Llandegla Moors to join the Clwydian Range, which eventually terminates in the limestone quarries above Prestatyn on the north coast.

Offa's Dyke follows the line of these hills. Constructed about AD 748 and running from Chepstow in South Wales, it follows roughly the present border until it crosses the River Dee down-stream from Llangollen, before climbing up and over Eglwyseg Mountain to World's End. It then heads north-west along the hills to Prestatyn. It is now a designated long distance footpath of 167 miles (269 km) and, though a shadow of its former self, can still be seen in several parts of these hills. At one time its massive earth work was 20 ft (6 m) wide, with a bank on one side 12 ft (4 m) high, and was probably designed more as a line of demarcation between the Mercian lands to the east and the Brythonic people to the west than a line of fortification, though the actual hills themselves must have been a daunting prospect. Wales is probably more Welsh to the west of it than to the east, and it is on the western side that the Welsh-speaking parts generally lie.

The main road (A494) from Chester to Corwen is one of the main access routes to North Wales and cuts across this range of hills from Mold through Loggerheads, a popular area for short walks, before crossing the shoulder of Moel Famau and dropping into the Vale of Clwyd at Ruthin.

Ruthin or Rudd-Din – meaning red fortress – is built on a small hill above the Afon Clwyd. It is notable for the remains of the castle, built above a red sandstone cliff near the centre of the town. The town probably grew around the castle, which was strategically placed to watch over the river and the road, which even in those days was one of the main routes from England. The original Welsh castle built by Prince Llewelyn's brother, Dafydd, was taken by Edward I in 1282 during the Welsh uprising and remained in English hands until dismantled as a Royalist stronghold by General Mytton in 1647 during the Civil War. **Ruthin Castle** now houses a luxury hotel.

A bypass has eased the congestion in the narrow streets and open square of the town centre. Two banks occupy the notable buildings on the main square. To the south a fine old black and white building is the former **Court House** dating from 1401, which served as both prison and courthouse. A short beam, which was once the gallows, still projects below the eaves. On the west

Places to Visit & Activities

In and Near Wrexham

Bersham Heritage Centre W

Bersham LL14 4HT
☎ 01978 261529
Industrial archaeology museum
relating to iron and coal.

Erddig Hall (NT) W

1 mile (1.6 km) south of Wrexham
off A438. LL13 0YT
☎ 01978 355314
Late seventeenth – and early
eighteenth-century mansion, features
include outbuildings, domestic
offices and portraits of staff. Original
furniture in main rooms. Large
gardens and parkland with Visitor
Centre.

Milestone Visitor Centre W

Bwlchgwyn Quarry, on A525
Wrexham-Ruthin Road. LL11 5UY
Geological Museum of Wales,
housing relics of distant and recent
past. Folk displays and trails.

St Giles Church W

Wrexham
Fine wrought iron gates dating from
1720. Decorated steeple, some
interesting contents within church.
Grave of Elihu Yale, benefactor of
Yale University.

Wrexham-Maelor Library and Art Centre W

Rhosddu Road, Wrexham
Has visiting exhibitions from
England and Wales.

Wrexham Tourist Information

Lampit Street, Wrexham
Open: 10–5pm (summer), 10–4pm
(winter).

Techniquest Plas Coch W

Mold Road, Wrexham
☎ 01978 293400
Discovery Centre. Over 60 hands on
exhibits & daily live science shows.

Grove Park Theatre W

Wrexham
☎ 01978 351091

Stiwt Theatre W

☎ 01978 841300

Odeon Cinema W

Plas Coch Road
☎ 01978 292093

Tea Dance Memorial Hall W

Wrexham
☎ 01978 292683
Open: Mon 2–4pm

Male Voice Choirs W

Visitors welcome to most rehersals
Brymbo male voice choir
☎ 01978 352898.
Froncysyltte choir
☎ 01978 361722.
Rhos male voice choir
☎ 01829 270210.

Please ring the choir first.

Cont'd on p60

The Horseshoe Pass on the A542 Llangollen-Ruthin road

The River Dee with the steam railway station at Llangollen

The Llangollen Canal by the National Eisteddfod Pavilion

side is the sixteenth-century **Exmewe Hall** in front of which is the **Maen Huail,** a stone on which King Arthur is said to have beheaded Huail, his rival in love. The hall was built by Thomas Exmewe, who later became Lord Mayor of London.

The **church of St Peter** stands to the north-east of the square. At one time it was a collegiate church, and dates in parts from the thirteenth and fourteenth centuries. The interior has a magnificent oak panelled roof, made of 500 carved panels, every one different, which was presented to all the men of Wales by Henry VII for their help in gaining the throne for him.

Ruthin stands at the head of the Vale of Clwyd, the river flowing north past the castle of Rhudlan to the sea close to Rhyl. Excavations have shown that the valley was occupied in 6000 BC and probably has been continuously since then.

Bersham Iron Works with the second oldest coke fired furnaces in the world

W = Suggestions for wet weather

Places to Visit & Activities

Country Parks:

Alynwaters
Mold Road, Gweryllt LL11 4AG
☎ 01978 763140

Minera Lead Mines & Country Park
☎ 01978 763140
Signposted Minera Lead Mines on A525.

Nantmill Visitor Centre
Rhosberse Road, Coed Poeth
☎ 01978 752772

Tymawr Country Park
Cae Gwilym Lane, Cefn Mawr LL14 3PT
☎ 01978 822780
countryparks@wrexham.gov.uk

Wrexham County MuseumW
County Buildings, Regent Street LL11 1RB
☎ 01978 317970

Wrexham Swimming Pool W
Bodhyfryd LL13 8DH
☎ 01978 297300

Golf Courses:

Claysfarm Golf Club
☎ 01978 661406

The Plassey Golf Course
Eyton
☎ 01978 780020

Wrexham Golf Club
☎ 01978 351476

In & Near Llangollen

Canal Exhibition Centre   W
Llangollen.
Models and films tell the story of growth and use of canals. Horse drawn boat trips. On canal just across road from main bridge.

Castell Dinas Bran
Thirteenth-century hilltop castle. Dominates the valley. Walk signposted from canal bridge on north side of river.

Chirk Castle   W
Half a mile (0.8 km) west of Chirk village. LL14 5AF
☎ 01691 777701
Calendar of events all year.
Large fortress partially converted to stately home. Fine furniture, tapestries and portraits. Formal gardens with clipped yews and flowering shrubs. Owned by National Trust.

Eliseg's Pillar
1,000-year-old pillar tells story of Eliseg, half a mile (0.8 km) up valley from Valle Crucis Abbey.

Horseshoe Falls
On Afon Dee 1 mile (1.6 km) east of town centre. Built by Telford to provide water for canal system.

Horseshoe Pass (NT)

On A542 Ruthin Road, 5 miles (8 km) north of Llangollen.
Steep climb with good views.

Llangollen Canal Cruises W

Horse Drawn Boat Co
Llangollen Wharf
☎ 01978 860702

Llangollen Motor Museum W

Pentrefelin.
Collection of yesteryear cars.

Llangollen Museum W

☎ 01978 862862

Llangollen Railway Society W

Railway Station, Llangollen.
Passenger trains now operate to Berwyn on the former Great Western Railway's Ruabon-Barmouth line. A varied collection of rolling stock and locomotives in the station and goods yard. By bridge across the river.

Plas Newydd

House of 'Ladies of Llangollen', beautiful black and white house in lovely gardens. South of river, well signposted.

Pontcysyllte Aqueduct W

Carries canal 120 ft (37 m) above Afon Dee, 1,000 ft (305 m) long. Superb position. Off Wrexham Road or from the A5.

Valle Crucis Abbey

1.5 miles (2.4 km) north of Llangollen on A542 to Ruthin. Substantial remains in a fine setting.

In & around Ruthin

Church of St Peter W

North-east corner of square. Fourteenth-century with magnificent panelled ceiling given to the men of Wales by Henry VII.

Court House

Stands in main square. Lovely black and white building, was old prison with gallows, now a bank.

Exmewe Hall

Opposite Court House. Built about 1500 by Thomas Exmewe, Lord Mayor of London. Now a bank.

Maen Huail

Large stone in front of Exmewe Hall on which King Arthur is reputed to have beheaded Huail, his rival in love.

Ruthin Castle

Norman castle with chequered history. Now a ruin and incorporated into an hotel.

Ruthin Craft Centre W

Park Road. Exhibition and workshops of many different crafts, which are worth seeing.

Ruthin Gaol W

Chapel Street, Ruthin
☎ 01824 708281
Houses local archives open to the public by appointment.

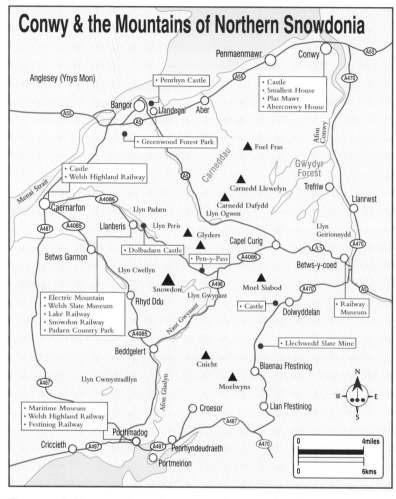

Conwy & the Mountains of Northern Snowdonia

Some visitors will perhaps explore only the resorts on the northern coast, but it is the mountains west of the River Conwy that are the attraction to many others. Rising steeply from the banks of the river, they are some of the highest peaks in England and Wales as well as some of the oldest. They are visible for many miles, and form a jagged skyline in sharp contrast to the surrounding moorlands.

For convenience the larger towns and villages will be visited first, for the hills are to a great extent the domain of the experienced climber and hill walker, though there are several interesting excursions on foot for the novice. All the large towns are situated on the coast and events have shown how important the routes along the coastal belt have been in the past. To the modern traveller they are equally important, for they are the normal access routes for most people approaching from the north and north-west of England. After passing through Abergele both coastal roads become one busy main road (A55), threading through Colwyn Bay and Llandudno Junction to arrive at one of the main crossing points of the Afon Conwy.

Conwy

There are three bridges across the Conwy estuary: Stephenson's tubular railway bridge of 1849, Telford's beautiful suspension bridge, which replaced an ancient and dangerous ferry and is now used only by pedestrians, and a modern road bridge which unfortunately had turned one of the most attractive historic towns in North Wales into a bottleneck for traffic during much of the summer. The suspension bridge, opened in 1826, was a major technical achievement of its time and was built by Thomas Telford, who was associated with many major transport projects in North Wales.

A road tunnel under the estuary was opened in 1991, bypassing the town altogether. The old town has now regained much of the peace and tranquillity of bygone days. Visitors must divert off this route at Llandudno Junction to visit the town.

The town of **Conwy** is situated on the very edge of the estuary with the superbly sited castle dominating the town from its rocky perch above the river. It is one of the most interesting, and probably one of the most visited towns in Wales. The walls surrounding the town are almost complete and with the castle form a unique defensive work. The enclosed narrow streets are busy as are the quay and landing stage; all contribute to make the town a popular holiday and yachting centre.

Conwy Castle is close to the site of a Cistercian monastery built in the tenth century. It was uprooted a hundred years later and moved to Maenan, 5miles (8km) upstream by Edward I, who saw the site as more suitable for defence than religion. The old abbey church survived and is now the parish church. The castle was built in only four years, a remarkable feat without modern mechanical aids, and served in part as a royal palace. During its stormy lifetime it has regularly changed hands between the Welsh and English before finally being captured by the Parliamentarians under General Mytton in 1646.

Modern visitors to the castle approach from Castle Square and it is from high on its walls that the best views of the nearby hills and the town walls can be seen. The walls were built at the same time as the castle and are part of an integral defensive scheme for the town; they follow the rise and fall of the land and are approximately 30 ft (9 m) tall with twenty-one towers throughout their length.

The quay is adjacent to the walls and

The Town of Conwy

Conwy's importance has always been as a port and crossing point of the river giving access to mountains which were the Welsh stronghold. When Edward 1 finally captured Conwy around 1280 he set about building a castle and a walled town to protect this major route. They were built as a single unit, the castle high on its rocky perch was intended to be a defensive work and a palace. It is known that Edward stayed in the castle several times and almost certainly on the way to Caernarfon to present his son to be the first English Prince of Wales.

The walls around the town were built at the same time as the castle and a wealthy town of merchants grew up inside the protection of the walls. Aberconwy House is the one remaining example of what the town must have looked like then. As a complete unit Conwy remains one of the finest walled towns in Europe.

has long been a port for fishing boats. Today it is becoming more important as a centre for yachtsmen and boating enthusiasts, the harbour providing a safe mooring. It is a busy place, full of hustle and bustle, though still a pleasant place to sit and watch the world go by. On the quayside is **Britain's smallest house**, a tiny half-up and half-down, built by a bachelor who obviously intended to remain so.

A new marina for 450 yachts has recently been opened downstream from the town with all the facilities needed these days. ☎ 01492 593000. A centre for the local mussel industry, with a fish shop, can be found on the quay.

Plas Mawr, built in 1576, is perhaps the most visited building after the castle. It is a fine example of an Elizabethan house, situated in the High Street, it has many interesting features both inside and outside. Several of the rooms have associations with Elizabeth I and the Lantern Room is reputed to be haunted. There are 365 windows and 52 doors in the house, coinciding with the

days and weeks of the year, a symbolic feature of which the Elizabethans were quite fond. Behind Plas Mawr is an art gallery well worth visiting, housing exhibitions of the **Royal Cambrian Academy of Art**, with all the best of Welsh painting and sculpture.

Lower down the High Street, **Aberconwy House** is a white timber and stone house owned by the National Trust. It is the only survivor of the type of medieval merchant's town house built in the fifteenth and sixteenth centuries, which formerly abounded in Conwy.

Almost surrounded by houses and streets stands St Mary's church, originally the abbey church. Much of the exterior structure is part of the original abbey, but the centuries have seen many additions to both inside and outside, and it is now a good example of the development of a parish church through the years. The churchyard includes the grave of two children who are celebrated in William Wordsworth's poem *We Are Seven*, which he wrote in 1798.

North Wales & Snowdonia

The smallest house in Great Britain on Conwy quay

Plas Mawr Honey Fair

The road, suspension and railway bridges, Conwy

The Groes Inn, the oldest licensed premises in Wales, on the B5106, just south of Conwy

Sychnant Pass near Conwy, with path to Conwy Mountain

The Menai Bridges

Thomas Telford proposed several schemes for crossing the Straits but eventually submitted a design in 1818 for a suspension bridge with a single span of 579 ft (177 m). There were to be 16 chains slung from piers 153 ft (47 m) above the high water and to carry two 12 ft (4 m) carriageways with a 6 ft (2 m) central walkway. Work started in 1819 and by 1825 the piers were complete and the chains were ready to be hauled into place, these were floated out on rafts and hauled up to be connected to those already slung over the piers. The roadways were added and the bridge was opened early the following year. Apart from some strengthening work of the cables in 1936 the bridge remains basically as it was then, a spectacular leap forward for civil engineering in a wonderful setting.

Some twenty years later a railway was proposed to link Holyhead with Chester and the rest of the country and the great railway engineer George Stephenson was given the task of surveying the route. Once again the daunting task of crossing the Menai had to be undertaken. At first he proposed adapting Telford's bridge and using horses to pull the trains across, this idea was soon dropped and again innovation proved the solution. To fit in with the Admiralty stipulation that there must be no hindrance to ships a tubular bridge was suggested and eventually accepted, and constructed a mile (1.6 m) along from the suspension bridge.

In 1845 Robert Stephenson, son of George Stephenson, was appointed Chief Engineer for the Chester-Holyhead Railway and he conceived the idea of a huge tubular bridge. Three stone piers were to be built and linked by steel rectangular section tubes and the railway would go inside them. Building them was a massive operation involving some techniques developed for that job. The central tubes were constructed on land by riveting together steel plates and joining sections together. They were floated out and raised up to the piers by hydraulic ram and then fixed in position. The piers are built of local white granite and in the tubes 2,000,000 rivets were used. Sadly in 1970 the original tubular bridge was set on fire by two boys searching for birds' eggs, The tubes with their large content of wood were destroyed. The reconstruction we see today incorporates both a road and a railway. It is therefore possible to see two wonders of the Industrial Revolution in the superb setting of North Wales.

Prehistoric sites

The hills to the south of the old and new roads have many reminders of the prehistoric people who inhabited the area. Just above Penmaenmawr at **Craiglwyd** was a stone axe factory. Using the tough granite, Stone Age man chipped and shaped it, both for his own use and for 'export'; axes from the site have been found all over Britain. There are many other prehistoric sites, some of which have been combined into a history trail from Penmaenmawr; leaflets are available in local shops.

Behind the town are some good hill walks with clear paths, particularly over **Conwy Mountain** (only 808 ft [246 m] high) to the Iron Age hillfort of **Caer Leion**. The old road crossed the **Sychnant Pass** behind Conwy to the coast at **Penmaenmawr**, and the head of the pass is a good place to park before enjoying one of the many short (or long) walks on the nearby slopes.

Conwy to Bangor

The river and the lakes upstream from Conwy are the breeding grounds for salmon. Several local families are licensed to catch the fish as they swim upstream, using nets that must not be below a particular mesh size, ensuring that only the larger fish are caught.

The modern road westwards from Conwy hugs the coast through a series of tunnels to give a smooth, quick ride through Penmaenmawr to Bangor.

The old road over **Sychnant Pass** had a formidable reputation and many travellers preferred to walk along the shoreline than cross the pass. Frequently the road was so bad that carriages had to be dismantled to get them over the worst parts.

Modern man still finds the granite worth quarrying, the summit of Penmaenmawr, from which the town gets its name, being a major source of this material; the height of the hill is reduced annually.

Aber, a short distance further on, is a small village known for the waterfall in the hills above. One turns off the main road and parks at the car park at the end of the valley. A walk of about a mile up the valley leads to the most impressive falls, which have a vertical drop of about 120 ft (37 m). To the west are the smaller cataracts of **Afon Bach**. The hills south of the falls are owned by the National Trust, and the mountains of the Carneddau are some of the wildest and highest in Snowdonia. Aber's car park is an ideal starting point for walks into these hills, but only experienced walkers, able to use a map and compass, should consider such an expedition.

The coast road continues south to join the A5 trunk road at Llandegai. This busy road from London to Holyhead was built by Thomas Telford in the early nineteenth century to speed the journey, and especially the Royal Mail, to and from Ireland. Opposite the junction is **Penrhyn Castle** and estate, now run by the National Trust. It was the home of the Pennant family who were the former owners of the Penrhyn Slate quarries in Bethesda.

Cwm Croesor and Cnicht

The old quarry buildings to Rhosydd Quarry above Cwm Croesor

Portmeirion (Photo Credit: www.portmeirion-village.com)

The house, which overlooks the Menai Strait, is a masterpiece of neo-Norman architecture and for obvious reasons slate has been used extensively both inside and outside.

The style and ostentatious design of the building reflect the unlimited amount of money available to many nineteenth-century businessmen. Parts of the building now house a doll museum, and on the estate is an industrial railway museum with locomotives and rolling stock from the Penrhyn and other slate quarries. In the old days, most of the slate shipped from the quarries went from the quay on the estate, so that the owner and management could keep a close eye on the amount being sold and dispatched. **Port Penrhyn** is signposted off the road into Bangor and remains much as it must have looked a century ago.

Bangor

Bangor, one of the old university towns of Wales, stands at the northern end of the **Menai Strait** most of the town being squeezed between two low hills in a shallow valley. It is dominated by the buildings of the **University College of North Wales,** which stand on the hill between the town and the Straits. The university is perhaps modern Bangor's main claim to fame, though in the past it has been a Celtic centre for Christianity; a bishopric was established here as long ago as AD 546.

Bangor Cathedral is thought to be the oldest in Britain in continuous use. The building, though not remarkable, has seen continuous development since Norman times and, despite suffering much at the hands of both Welsh and English aggressors, its history seems to consist of being regularly burnt down and rebuilt. The exterior of the building still shows signs of these regular conflagrations and there is much evidence of the many phases of its development. Restoration was begun in 1866 under the care of Sir George Gilbert Scott, who approached it with an eye to the past and was able to include much detail that had been destroyed in previous centuries. Nearby is the old **Bishop's Palace**, built mainly in the sixteenth century and now the town hall.

Almost opposite is the **Theatr Gwynedd**, the centre for the performing arts in the county. The **Museum of Welsh Antiquities**, housed in the Old Canonry near the cathedral, contains exhibits from prehistoric, Roman and more recent times giving a good background to the development of the town, surrounding area and Wales generally. The city was a quiet religious centre until early last century. The opening of the two bridges across the Menai Strait in the first half of the nineteenth century resulted in increased traffic by road and rail through the town. With the arrival of the university college in 1883, Bangor finally became a municipality and busy commercial centre.

Menai Strait to Caernarfon

Visitors may prefer to follow the A5 trunk road, which misses the centre of Bangor. One little delight on the quayside is the refurbished pier stretching into the Menai Strait; worth stopping here if only to stretch the legs and walk along a genuine Victorian pier with wonderful views along the Strait. The Strait, which divide Anglesey from the mainland, vary between 200 yd (183 m) and a mile (1.6 km) wide and are 13 miles (21 km) long. They have formed an almost impenetrable barrier for most invaders and travellers until the first road bridge was constructed in the early in nineteenth century.

The Menai Strait, though narrow, are notorious for the tides that race through them and which made the crossing extremely hazardous and fraught with difficulty. At one time there were seven ferries all overcharging for the short trip. The most common route was on foot across the Lavan Sands just north of Bangor and then by ferry across the remaining water to Beaumaris (Biwmares) on Anglesey. Cattle going to market on the mainland were forced to swim across, urged on by drovers in boats but losses were high and even that crossing was dangerous for all travellers.

Many ideas had been proposed for a safe crossing including an embankment with a drawbridge to allow the passage of shipping, the Admiralty insisting there should be no hindrance to the passage of fully rigged ships. It formed a major obstacle to the completion of Telford's 268 mile (431 km) road from London to Holyhead (A5) mentioned in an earlier chapter. The great engineer that he was, he solved the many problems admirably with only the second suspension bridge ever to be built and in 1825 when the bridge was opened the Straits could be crossed safely by man and beast for the first time in history.

After leaving the bridges behind the road south moves a little inland before

Investitures

Traditionally the castle is where Edward II was invested as the first Prince of Wales after his birth there in 1284. The castle has in more recent times seen the investitures as Prince of Wales of the future Edward VIII (in 1911) and of Prince Charles (in 1969).

passing above **Portdinorwic**. In the heyday of the slate quarries a narrow gauge railway came down from Llanberis to load the waiting ships with cut slates at this tiny port. Neglected for many years it has taken on a new life and is now a popular centre for yachting and holidays.

Caernarfon

At the southern end of the Menai Strait is the historic town of **Caernarfon**. It is probably the best known of all the towns in North Wales, and stands in a magnificent position at the foot of the mountains overlooking Anglesey. The castle, built by Edward I, is one of the greatest (and most attractive) castles in the country. It stands above the busy quayside as a reminder of the strategic importance of this bustling town.

Unusually, the castle has thirteen polygonal towers and banded masonry and although outwardly perfect it is internally just a shell. Like all castles in this region it has had a stormy career, playing a significant part in the wars between the Welsh and English princes. It was twice unsuccessfully besieged by Owain Glyndwr; in the Civil War it

Above: Caernarfon Castle from the quay

Right: Construction of the Welsh Highland Railway between Waunfawr and Betws Garmon

Below: The Welsh Highland Railway's new station (2002) at Waunfawr. You can catch the train at Caernarfon for a trip into Snowdonia

Snowdon from near Rhyd-Ddu

stood for the king, and when captured by Cromwell's troops in 1660 the order was given to destroy it. This warrant was fortunately never exercised and it stands now as a magnificent reminder of the castle builder's craft. In the Queen's Tower within the walls is the **Museum of the Royal Welch Fusiliers**, with many mementoes from the history of the regiment.

As at Conwy, much of the town wall survives, built with the castle as part of an integrated defensive system. It surrounds the old parts of the town, the narrow streets forming a regular pattern within. In the north-west corner, and built into the walls, is the **chantry of St Mary** which utilised the adjoining tower as a vestry and bell tower. There are many fine old buildings enclosed by the walls, including the **Black Buoy Inn**, a traditional public house with some good local dishes, and the **old Market Hall** which now is more a centre for local crafts than a market.

Until very recently the town, like many along the coast, was blighted by traffic, but the building of a bypass has considerably relieved the congestion, thus allowing visitors to wander at a more leisurely pace around this lovely little town. **Castle Square** with its **statue of Lloyd George** is now relatively free from traffic; it has a Saturday market and is an ideal base from which to explore.

The Romans also appreciated the value of the site's strategic importance, or perhaps they just found it slightly less hostile than the mountains inland. They built a fort, known as **Segontium**, just to the south of the present town, half a mile (0.8 km) out, on the road to Beddgelert. Little now remains but the foundations give a good idea of the ground plan. On the site is the excellent **Segontium Roman Museum** covering the history of the fort and the organization of the Roman army in Britain and other related subjects. The fort was occupied from about AD 78 to AD 380 when the Roman troops began to withdraw from Britain. During that time a sizeable community had grown up outside the walls and on retirement many of the soldiers are believed to have settled and farmed in the area. It was a fort well integrated with local life.

The view south from Caernarfon and Bangor is of the mountains. They are not large by comparison with other European mountain ranges but they always give an overriding impression of grandeur. They form the northern end of the Snowdonia National Park and are divided into three distinct ranges, separated by deep valleys. To the east, bounded on one side by the Conwy Valley and on the other by the Nant Ffrancon Pass, are the Carneddau; in the centre are the Glyders; and on the west, the highest of all, is Snowdon with its surrounding massif. In all there are fourteen peaks over 3,000 ft (914 m), all linked by footpaths.

The mountains

The mountains, originally formed more than 300 million years ago, are the worn down remains of much higher mountains. They have been folded by earth movements to more than 20,000 ft (6,096 m) and then gradually worn by changing temperatures, water and ice, to their present size. The valleys have been carved by ancient glaciers

Legends of Snowdon

This is the land of the legendary King Arthur. Yr Wyddfa, the highest peak, is traditionally the tomb of Rhita Fawr slain by Arthur. Arthur is supposed to have fought his last battle at the Pass of Arrows (Bwlch y Saethau) below Snowdon's summit; Llyn Llydaw by tradition is the lake into which Excalibur was thrown. On the slopes above is a cave in which three of King Arthur's knights rest, ready to come to the aid of the country when needed.

and many of the hanging valleys, called cwms, have been dammed by glacial deposits to hold lakes. The debris of glaciers is scattered around the hillsides and in moraines along and across the valleys. The alpine plants left by the receding ice in some of the high cwms provide a living link with the Ice Age and show how little these mountains have changed despite man's interference. They were also the reason the first tourists came in search of rare plant species.

Snowdon

Snowdon is the highest mountain in England and Wales. With its sharp ridges and sombre cwms, it is inevitable that stories have grown around it.

Despite the legends, what is more certain is that several of the Welsh princes retreated into the area when defeated, for it proved a most hostile environment to the pursuing English troops.

The Snowdon Massif, known more traditionally by the Welsh as **Yr Eryri**, is a star-shaped cluster of peaks connected by a series of steep ridges, the highest, **Snowdon** or **Yr Wyddfa** at 3,560 ft (1085 m), is in the centre and generally the object of most people's attention. The main routes to the summit are fairly easy underfoot though can be arduous to those unused to hill walking. Many thousands reach the summit each year, though to enjoy the walk a certain amount of fitness is recommended.

North of Yr Wyddfa is the summit of **Crib-y-Ddysgl** (3,493 ft [1,065 m]) leading out on the narrow ridge to **Crib Goch** (3,023 ft [921 m]) in the northeast. This is a splendid ridge to walk with towering pinnacles and buttresses and with superb situations, but is not for the inexperienced or faint hearted.

To the south-east is the craggy ridge of **Lliwedd** (2,497 ft [761 m]) with its steep walls overlooking **Llyn Llydaw**, and looking south is the long southern ridge leading out to **Yr Aran** (2,451 ft [747 m]) above the Gwynant Valley. There are good tracks across the ridges but care must be taken as the weather can be extremely inclement with gusting winds.

Many visitors are content to reach the summit by the rack-and-pinion **Snowdon Railway**, which ascends the 5 miles (8 km) from Llanberis, with fantastic views en route. For those who achieve the summit by whatever means the views, providing the weather is clear, are worth the effort. You are above every other mountain in England and Wales and can see many of them; the Welsh mountains and lakes are immediately obvious even down to Cadair Idris 30 miles (48 km) to the south. Further

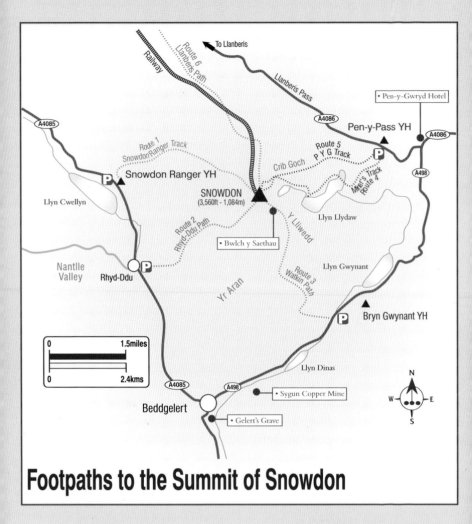

Footpaths to the Summit of Snowdon

afield to the west the Wicklow Hills of Ireland can be seen, visibility permitting, across the sea and to the north the Isle of Man and the Lake District, with the coast of Lancashire and Blackpool Tower supposedly visible. For more distant views a clear day and a good imagination is needed. There is a café and bar on the summit to reward thirsty walkers but be warned that it is only open when the train is running.

The ascent of the summit, Yr Wyddfa,

has understandably been a popular achievement, at least from early last century when George Borrow in his book *Wild Wales* describes how he walked up with his family in 1850 and even at that time 'there was a rude cabin in which refreshments are sold and in which a person resides throughout the year'.

There are six main routes up Snowdon, starting from car parks all around the mountain. Although some are easier and some are longer, all require much physical effort and a sound knowledge of mountain walking, for the weather can change drastically during the 5–8 hours of the walk. All the paths are well made and quite easy to follow if care is taken.

Perhaps the greatest expedition is the **Snowdon Horseshoe**, a traverse of all the main peaks to and from Pen-y-Pass. It involves steep climbing and knife-edge ridges following the rim of the cwm surrounding Llyn Llydaw and taking in the summits of Crib-Goch, Crib-y-Ddysgl, over Yr Wyddfa before descending to Bwlch-y-Saethau and the steep crags of Lliwedd and thence back down the Miners' Track to Pen-y-Pass. **It must be stressed that this is a major undertaking and should not be attempted without a stout pair of boots, a head for heights and much previous experience; the weather and rock conditions**

Footpaths to the Summit of Snowdon

Route 1

Snowdon Ranger Track: 3.75 miles (6 km). An easy path with delightful views, zig-zags above youth hostel.

Route 2

Rhyd-Ddu Path: 3.75 miles (6 km). Easy to follow, climbs gradually to summit, Steeper near top.

Route 3

Watkin Path: 3.5 miles (5.6 km). Most interesting, but hardest walk. Good path at first up to Bwlch y Saethau, steep and loose after that. A long climb.

Route 4

Miner's Track: 3.75 miles (6 km). Follows copper miners' track to lake, then rises more steeply to join PYG (Pen-y-Gwryd) track to summit. Good for introduction to the mountain if you do not wish to go to the top.

Route 5

PYG Track: 3.25 miles (5.2 km). Good route. Climbs quickly and then contours around cwm. Zig-zags below summit. A well-made path. Recommended favourite route.

Route 6

Llanberis Path: 5 miles (8 km). Follows close to railway. Starts in Llanberis and climbs gradually. Not the most interesting route. Easy but long.

Ensure you are well prepared for the climb; with suitable footwear, wet weather gear, food & drink and suitable maps. Check the weather before setting off, allow adequate time to do the climb in daylight and avoid Route 5 if you suffer from vertigo!

should be checked before attempting this marvellous expedition.

Llanberis to Ogwen

Pen-y-Pass, the highest point of the **Llanberis Pass**, and the starting point for many of the Snowdon walks, is the site of the old Gorphwysfa Hotel, an old coaching inn converted some years ago to a Youth Hostel. In the early part of the century the hotel was the centre for the pioneer rock climbers who visited the many crags on the slopes of Snowdon. The road descends steeply from there down to the south-east to the **Pen y Gwryd Hotel**, which superseded it as the meeting place for climbers. Both the Youth Hostel and the hotel are Mountain Rescue points. To the north of Pen-y-Pass the road winds down the Llanberis Pass, between the huge rock buttresses which are the playgrounds of the modern rock climbers, to Llyn Peris and Llyn Padarn.

Llyn Peris has recently been drained and dammed to form the bottom lake of the huge **Dinorwig Pump Storage Power Station**. This hydro-electric scheme involves the use of two lakes, one high lake and one lower reservoir. The top lake, Marchlyn Mawr, behind Elidir Fawr to the north, stores the water until generating capacity is needed. The water is then released and drives the turbines built under the hillside opposite and flows into the lower lake, Llyn Peris. During off peak times, using surplus electricity from the National Grid, the water is then pumped back to the higher lake for future use.

It is a massive project involving deep underground workings and tunnels, well hidden in the slate quarries and underground, but the entrance to the power station is visible across Llyn Peris. The electricity is fed into the national grid. See the Visitor Centre at Electric Mountain on the main road through Llanberis.

Llanberis, in the bottom of the valley, sits almost between the two lakes and is probably best known as the starting point for the Snowdon Mountain Railway. This is a rack-and-pinion railway carrying passengers to the summit of Snowdon; as an easy alternative to walking, it is very popular. Not far from the station is the **National Slate Museum**, with exhibits and buildings relating to all aspects of quarry work. The **old quarry railway** has been rebuilt to provide a pleasant run along the north shore of **Llyn Padarn** through a **country park** of the same name. It is a narrow gauge railway and many of the original locomotives are still in use.

On a small hill above the town sits the round keep of **Dolbadarn Castle** built in the early thirteenth century, it is thought for Llewelyn The Great, while on the opposite side of the lake can be seen the huge tiers of the old **Dinorwig Slate Mine** which rise for 1,500 ft (457 m) up the side of the mountain. The mine now houses the aforementioned Pump Storage Power Station.

To the north of the town and above the massive slate tips rise the bulky slopes of Elidir Fawr and the Glyder range of mountains, most of which are over 3,000 ft (914 m) high. They are accessible on foot from the Llanberis side, but the most interesting walks and ascents are made from the north, starting mainly from **Llyn Ogwen**, where there are several convenient car parks. There is no village at **Ogwen** just a collection of buildings comprising a Youth Hostel and an adventure school – but it is easy to get the feel of the high mountains despite the busy main road.

The old packhorse road runs parallel to the modern road, this is part of Telfords London – Holyhead road, and can be traced for much of the distance along the valley side. It makes a fine walk in magnificent surroundings and is fairly level and easy to follow. The remains of the old packhorse bridge can be seen underneath the more modern road bridge by the falls below Llyn Ogwen.

The Glyders

Access to the **Glyders** is by a footpath that climbs steeply from behind **Ogwen Cottage**, a Mountain Rescue Post,

before levelling out into **Cwm Idwal**. The path then follows the shores of Llyn Idwal past the **Idwal Slabs**, birthplace of rock climbing as a sport in this country. It then climbs steeply to **Twll Du or Devil's Kitchen,** a narrow defile of black rock, which seems to cut the mountain in half.

The whole of Cwm Idwal is a nature reserve with many rare species of alpine plants and orchids found amongst the rocks. It was the early botanists who started rock climbing as they searched higher and higher for new specimens. A pleasant afternoon can be enjoyed without leaving the cwm but the higher mountains are steep and rocky, though in many respects totally different from their neigh-bours.

Climbing on past Devil's Kitchen the path comes to a small lake (Llyn-y-Cwn) and then divides. To the right the track climbs easily to the summit of **Y Garn** (3,104 ft [946 m]) then along the crest to **Mynydd Perfedd** and either west above **Marchlyn Mawr**, the top lake of the pump storage scheme,

Dinorwig Slate Quarry

Dinorwig Slate Quarry can be seen towering above Llyn Peris, the slate was extracted by the open terrace method where the rock was drilled, a charge of black powder was inserted and huge rectangular pieces of rock were blasted from the quarry face.

The blocks were then moved by horse-drawn truck to a working area were they were sawn and split and trimmed into slates. The men worked in small independent groups and were paid on what they produced. The work was hazardous particularly in the mines where the added danger was obviously the dark. Many of the men that worked the slate quarries scattered throughout these hills did not live locally and would trek over the hills to work on a Monday morning with their few belongings and the food for the week and then return to their families at weekend.

The Electric Mountain Exhibit

Snowdon Ranger Youth Hostel, the start of one of the routes up the mountain

Above: Conwy Castle

Left: The National Slate Museum, Llanberis

The Ugly House on the A5 between Betws-y-coed and Capel Curig

to **Elidir Fawr** (3,029 ft [923 m]) or north to **Carnedd-y-Filiast** and down into Bethesda.

Taking the track on the left from Llyn-y-Cwn and going south-east, the path rises steeply up the scree-covered slopes of **Glyder Fawr** (3,279 ft [999 m]) to the summit, a rather desolate boulder-strewn plateau. It continues along the ridge past the well-named **Castell-y-Gwynt** (Castle of the Winds) to **Glyder Fach** (3,262 ft [994 m]) and the flat stone of the Cantilever, a perched block, which seems delicately balanced but has so far defied all the efforts of large and small parties to dislodge it.

The views from both these summits are some of the finest in Snowdonia, looking down on the surrounding mountains and valleys, with the summit of **Tryfan** seemingly only a step away to the east. The path descends steeply alongside the **Bristly Ridge** to the cwm and then north back to Ogwen.

However the summit of Tryfan (3,010 ft [917 m]), only a short scramble above, is well worth the extra effort, for this is one of the true mountains of North Wales. With a sharp profile from every viewpoint it stands separated from all others above the valley. On this ascent one's hands will be needed for extra grip, as the path to the top is steep and rocky. The summit is crowned by two great monoliths, imaginatively known as **Adam and Eve**. They are close together and it is said that a true Welsh mountaineer is one who has stepped from one to the other. With the steep drop below it is safer not to attempt it, but to descend by the much slower, but safer, route back to the cwm, and then north down to Ogwen Cottage.

The Carneddau

Between the Nant Ffrancon Pass and Llyn Ogwen and the Conwy Valley is the largest range of hills, the **Carneddau**, which rise steeply above the lake mainly north from **Pen-yr-Oleu-Wen** (3,211 ft [979 m]) to **Drum** (2,529 ft [771 m]), then sloping more gently on the east to the foothills above Conwy. They are of a completely different character, being more rounded and grass-covered, with only occasional steep cliffs and cwms. The walking is more arduous and the route finding more difficult. As it is a large area with many access points, it is suggested that those considering mountain walking here should equip themselves with a large scale map to gain maximum enjoyment.

Despite this advice, it would be unfair not to give at least a brief description of these hills. The main path ascends from the west end of Llyn Ogwen and rises very steeply for almost 2,000 ft (610 m) to the summit of Pen-yr-Oleu-wen. Once this has been achieved, there is little further climbing for the whole length of the ridge. Circling round the very edge of one of the most perfect cwms, Ffynnon Lloer, the summit of **Carnedd Dafydd** (3,427 ft [1045 m]) is soon reached; then on to **Carnedd Llewelyn** (3,458 ft [1054 m]). From there a spur goes east providing some interesting and mainly downhill walking, and for those who have had enough there is a circular return route to the valley. Going north from Carnedd Llewelyn, the ridge can be followed over **Foel Grach** (3,196

The Snowdon Mountain Railway

This was suggested first in the early 1890s, and work began in 1894 to a Swiss design. The rack and pinion railway with a maximum gradient of 20% was built by a British firm and the locomotives by a Swiss company. It was completed in remarkably quick time and opened in 1896. The first train made a successful ascent; unfortunately the second left the track on the descent and a passenger was killed. The line was modified and there have since been no serious accidents.

Seven locomotives are in use, five built before 1900 and two in 1923, all burn coal 5–7 cwts (254–355 kg) in a single journey. Sixty passengers can be carried in the seven compartments per trip.

ft [974 m]), **Foel Fras** and then down to Drum. This is a full day's excursion, and it is best to arrange transport at the northern end, if a long walk back is to be avoided.

The smaller hills to the south of the main range are split by a series of deep valleys, each containing a lake of individual character dammed to provide water for industry in the Conwy Valley. The northernmost, **Llyn Eigau**, burst its dam in 1925 causing a disastrous flood; the great masonry blocks and deep fissure created can be seen just below the remaining lake. The next, **Llyn Cowlyd**, is set in bleak uplands, while the two smaller ones to the south, **Llyn Crafnant** and **Llyn Geirionnydd**, are in wooded valleys. The latter is a popular spot for day trippers, yachtsmen and water skiers, though the roar of power boats upsets the serenity of this beautiful spot. All these valleys, with the exception of Cowlyd, can be reached easily by road from the Conwy Valley.

South of Snowdon

To the south is the **Gwydyr Forest** stretching from Llyn Crafnant to Pen-machno and covering many of the hills and valley sides. The forests have been developed since 1921 by the Forestry Commission and are now a Forest Park with free access. They are a fine introduction to the wilder mountains beyond.

There are many footpaths through the forest, some following long forgotten roads to old lead mines and quarries, while others follow delightful little streams to quiet mountain lakes. Everybody is welcome provided that they respect the forest and natural environment. As the forest has many old copper and lead mines, care must be taken when walking near the shafts.

Betws-y-coed to Capel Curig

The small town of **Betws-y-coed** is almost surrounded by the forest at the junction of three valleys, the Lledr Valley from the south, the Llugwy Valley from the west and the Conwy Valley to the north. It sits astride the A5 trunk road and is a frequent bottleneck in summer as most of the traffic has to cross the graceful **Waterloo Bridge**.

Beddgelert

This cast iron bridge was built in 1815 and carries the inscription in large letters: 'This Arch was Constructed in the Same Year the Battle of Waterloo was Fought', as well as decorative flowers in the spandrels. There are hotels, cafés and many craft shops, while near the railway station is the **Conwy Valley Railway Museum**.

The Tourist Information Centre has descriptive leaflets of the many short walks in the locality and in the nearby forest.

The main road rises through the town and just on the left is an old stone bridge with a small cataract below it, if you are lucky you may see salmon jumping. A few miles upstream and next

Llyn Geirionydd; whether you want to walk around the lake or picnic at the carpark, it's worth seeking out

Llyn Dinas, on the A498, south of Snowdon looking towards Cnicht

The Conwy Estuary from the quayside at Conwy, looking towards Deganwy

to the road, are the **Swallow Falls**, a magnificent sight particularly after rainfall. The next village, **Capel Curig**, is merely a cross roads with a few climbing and other shops and several hotels.

Climb Moel Siabod

The imposing mountain across the lake is **Moel Siabod**; from this side it is one of the easier mountain walks. Start about one mile towards Betws-y-Coed at Pont Cyfyng where a small road turns off to a cluster of cottages. The main track begins there and follows an old quarry road which at first rises easily past the slate quarries and then follows the ridge with some easy scrambling to the grass slopes below the rocky summit cairn. There are fine views over the sheer drop to the cwm below. The path along and down the ridge to the Pen-y-Gwryd Hotel gives a long walk; it is best to return the way you came for the views are always different on the way back.

Just outside Capel Curig is **Plas-y-Brenin**, the National Mountaineering Centre, which provides courses in all grades of walking, climbing and skiing in the surrounding mountains, and canoeing on the nearby lake and river. The centre is open to the public with indoor climbing walls and at the back a dry ski slope. Many courses are introductory and even the most inexperienced can participate.

Past Plas-y-Brenin the road skirts the shores of **Llynau Mymbyr** and continues up the long glaciated valley with one of the finest views of Snowdon directly ahead. Looking into the horse-shoe formed by the Crib Goch ridge to the right and Lliwedd to the left you look directly up to the majestic summit in the centre; from here it always looks forbidding and sombre.

Nant Gwynant

Coming to the junction at the Pen-y-Gwryd Hotel continue ahead to Nant Gwynant, the road to the right going over Pen-y-Pass and thence to the Llanberis Pass. This comfortable hotel was the training headquarters for the first successful team to conquer Mount Everest in 1953. The main room in the bar has the signatures of these climbers on the ceiling. Across the road on a small hillock is the square base of a Roman fort, which controlled the ancient routeways over this pass, though a less hospitable posting could hardly be found for men brought up on the Mediterranean coast.

The road ahead descends easily to Nant Gwynant passing a viewpoint on the right. It is worth a stop for perhaps the finest view of Snowdon and the valley. Below is **Llyn Gwynant** above the brooding shape of Yr Wyddfa. Continuing on you pass Llyn Gwynant, with its canoeists and windsurfers and **Llyn Dinas**, always quiet and peaceful and after a few miles arrive at the lovely village of **Beddgelert**.

Between Llyn Gwynant and Beddgelert is the **Sygun Copper Mine**, which has been reopened as a visitor attraction. Visitors are taken along levels and up ladderways, rediscovering the old passageways, which had been abandoned so long ago. On the surface it is possible to see the remains of some of the old buildings, reclaimed from a dense rhododendron undergrowth. There is a small café here and video-corner where details of the mine and its reopening may be seen.

Beddgelert

Standing at the confluence of two rivers that join to become the Afon Glaslyn, Beddgelert is a bustling village torn between the tourist trade and the chaos the traffic it brings can cause. It is nevertheless relatively unspoilt and at the heart of the mountains.

Beddgelert is an ideal centre for exploring the surrounding hills, for there are some fine hotels and guest houses; though a little crowded in summer, it has a charm of its own. The old Welsh Highland Railway passed close to the village.

There are several easy strolls from the village, the most popular to Gelert's Grave just a short distance along the south bank of the river, now well paved and accessible with a pushchair. After visiting the grave you can continue along the path but must return the same way. Crossing the Iron Bridge in the village to the opposite bank of the river gives a similar easy walk along the riverbank to the delightful Aberglaslyn Pass, with some places to paddle or throw stones in the stream.

Should you wish to extend your walk to three miles and enjoy a lovely but easy walk the path descends to river level and follows the old fisherman's path along the riverside, safe but exciting to Aberglaslyn Bridge, probably the most photographed river view in Britain and justifiably so. Turn left and a footpath leads over to the car park at the bottom of Cwm Bychan, from here

you can head up the valley to perhaps one of the nicest but easiest walks in the area, as you rise the mountains around come into view with Cnicht and the Moel-wyns rising grandly to the left and to the south the estuary of the Glaslyn, Traeth Mawr. Continuing upwards brings you to the old remains of the copper mines and the pylons that carried the ore in a bucket conveyor down to the roadway. Above the last mine and just below the head of the cwm a path leads of to the left past a small lake and over the ridge where a steep but easy descent down the old miners track will bring you to the Sygun Copper Mine where you can join the road and turn left to meander easily back to Beddgelert and some well deserved refreshment.

Aberglaslyn to the Moelwyns

South of Beddgelert, and downstream, is the well known **Aberglaslyn Pass**, which must feature more often on calendars than any other place in Wales. It has all the components of a classic beauty spot. A steep sided valley, trees, a tumbling river and a bridge all combine perfectly and can be viewed with little effort from the roadside. At one time ships could sail right up to the bridge, but since the building of the embankment across the mouth of the estuary, the land has been reclaimed and the river is impassable from Porthmadog.

The hills to the east of Aber-glaslyn are fairly easily accessible on minor roads which branch off the main road from there to Penrhyndeudraeth. The first road up the Nantmor valley has several picnic spots and small parking areas; it is a beautiful area, but the road is narrow. From the high point on that road, where there is an old slate quarry, a good little path opposite a white cottage goes up to **Llyn Llagi**. The path continues beyond the lake and over the shoulder to **Llyn-yr-Adar** and on to the ridge of **Cnicht**. This can be traversed with wonderful views of the estuary and descended until the path breaks off to the right at a col below a small crag. It joins an old packhorse trail, which if followed to the right, goes downhill to the road following a lovely little stream back to the quarry. Several other footpaths leave this road for other lakes, and they are all fairly easy walking but as they may be damp underfoot, it is best to go well shod.

Cnicht, sometimes called the Matterhorn of North Wales, is best seen from the south, and with **Moelwyn Bach** and **Moelwyn Mawr** it stands proudly above the estuary. **Croesor**, a small village at the end of a minor road, is the starting point for any walks on that range. The road to Croesor starts by a large gatehouse in **Llanfrothen**. It is narrow and high walled and passes **Plas Brodanw**, home of the late Sir Clough Williams-Ellis the architect, best known for the hotel and village

Interior view of Caernarfon Castle

Llechwedd, Slate Mine (Photo Credit: Llechwedd Slate Mine)

Looking up Duffryn Mymbyr to the Snowdon horseshoe

of Portmeirion. Opposite the house a gate leads uphill to a small castle with superb views over the estuary; it is a 'folly', being the architect's wedding present from his brother officers during his time in the army. It is a short but very pleasant stroll.

Sir Clough Williams-Ellis

He was perhaps best known locally for his style of dress, always plus fours and yellow socks, though more famous for his creation of **Portmeirion** the village where the cult TV series *The Prisoner* was filmed. The Italianate village is based around a hotel on the estuary of Traeth Bach in a delightful setting, there are shops, a café and it is open to visitors. He is also renowned as an architect for his individual style mainly Classical and Georgian.

From the car park at Croesor there is a well signposted track that follows the ridge to the top of Cnicht. It is an easy walk, with one difficult scrambling section just below the summit, but if care is taken it should present no problems. The walk is recommended for its ease and views.

Moelwyn Mawr is best tackled by following the old quarry road beyond the village to the highest quarry, which until recently had a fine collection of buildings still surviving. From the back of the quarry the footpath up and over the shoulder brings one to the top, before descending down the ridge to the south and directly to the village.

Moelwyn Bach, the smaller of the two, can be approached from the south through a small forestry plantation at the high point of the road linking Croesor and Rhyd. The path is not too clear and it is wet underfoot, but once the ridge is reached walking is drier and straightforward; the views from the summit are magnificent. For ease it is suggested that the descent is made by the same route.

There are many fine walks in this area and it is ideal for a good day out. There are also numerous abandoned quarries and slate mines to interest the industrial archaeologist. These hills are less frequented than those to the north, but there is still much to see and enjoy, though proper dress and equipment are essential.

The Legend of Gelert

The village thrives on the story of the legendary Gelert, a dog belonging to Prince Llewelyn, which he slew after returning from a hunting trip on finding that his son was missing and the dog was covered in blood. It was only later that his son was found safe and a wolf dead nearby, obviously killed by the dog. He buried the faithful hound and the 'grave' is just a short stroll alongside the river from the village centre. A similar story appears in other parts of the world, and it is most likely that it was introduced here by an over-zealous publican in the eighteenth century to encourage visitors. It is more probable that the Gelert referred to in the village name was an early Christian connected with a priory which once stood on that site.

Places of Interest & Activities

Conwy Area

Aberconwy House (NT) W

Castle Street, Conwy LL32 8AY
☎ 01492 592246
A good example of a fourteenth-century timber framed house. Houses Conwy Exhibition, depicting life of the town from Roman Times.

Bodnant Garden (NT)

Tal-y-Cafn LL28 5RE
☎ 01492 650460
See Chapter 3 for more details.

Conwy Castle and Walls

LL32 8LY
☎ 01492 592358
Magnificent setting, best example in country.

Conwy Countryside Service

☎ 01492 575290
Provide leaflets describing walks, trails & pathways

Conwy Estuary RSPB Nature Reserve

Entrance off roundabout, junction 18, A55.
☎ 01492 584091
A great place to see local birds and wildlife. Coffee shop, nature trails.
www.rspb.org.uk/conwy

Conwy Estuary Trips

Riverbus
☎ 01492 592830

Conwy Mountain

Hut circles and footpaths in most directions.

Plas Mawr W

High Street, Conwy LL32 8DE
☎ 01492 580167
Perfect example of Elizabethan building. Now houses Royal Cambrian Academy of Art at the rear.

St Mary's Church W

Conwy
Originally part of Cistercian Abbey but developed as a parish church over the years.

Smallest House

Britain's smallest house, on the quayside.

Sychnant Pass

Old road connecting Conwy and Penmaenmawr.

Trefriw Woollen Mills W

Conwy Valley, Trefriw LL27 0NQ
☎ 01492 640462

Conwy Suspension Bridge (NT) W

By the castle LL32 8LD
☎ 01492 573282

Cont'd overleaf

W = Suggestions for wet weather

Places of Interest & Activities

Bangor Area

Bangor Cathedral

Thought to be the oldest in Britain, shows evidence of continuous development since sixth century.

Gwynedd Museum & Art Gallery   W

Ffordd Gwynedd, Bangor LL57 1DT

Greenwood Forest Park

Nr Bangor LL56 4QN
☎ 01248 670076

Old Canonry   W

Bangor. Houses Museum of Welsh Antiquities, with collection of seventeenth-century furniture illustrating Welsh rural crafts. Prehistoric and Romano-British objects.

Penrhyn Castle (NT)   W

Just off the A55 north of Bangor. LL57 4HN
☎ 01248 353084
An elegant neo-Norman mansion on the edge of the Menai Strait; many slate artefacts in the building. Doll museum and industrial railway museum. Formal Vixtorian walled garden.

Caernarfon

Aviation Museum

Dinas Dinlle LL54 5TP
☎ 01286 830800

Caernarfon airport

Pleasure flights

Caernarfon Castle

Castle Street LL55 2AY
☎ 01286 677617
Finest of Edward's castles.
Polygonal towers with banded
masonry make it unique.

Electric Mountain   W

Llanberis LL55 4UR
☎ 01286 870636

Fun Centre   W

Caernarfon LL55 1AR
☎ 01286 671911

Inigo Slate Works   W

Caernarfon LL54 7UE
☎ 01286 830242

Market Hall   W

Near town centre, Caernarfon
Now a centre for local crafts and
shops.

Museum of Royal Welch
Fusiliers   W

☎ 01286 673362
Military museum inside castle, with
many mementoes of the regiment's
past.

Town Walls

Caernarfon
Circle inner part of town,
part of integral defensive system.

Segontium

Beddgelert Road, Caernarfon
☎ 01286 675625
Roman Fort on outskirts of town.
Some buildings and a museum
showing history of the site.

Llanberis Area

Beacon Climbing
Centre   W

Ceunant, Nr Llanberis LL55 4SA
☎ 0845 450 8222

Dinorwig Power Station/
Electric Mountain   W

Llanberis LL55 4UR
☎ 01286 870636
Information centre, huge cavern
inside mountain with guided tours.

Dolbadarn Castle

Home of the Welsh Princes in the
twelfth century, it stands above the
lake guarding the entrance to the
Llanberis Pass.

*Left: Padarn
Country Park*

Cont'd overleaf

W = Suggestions for wet weather

Places of Interest & Activities

Llanberis Lake Railway W

LL55 4TY

☎ 01286 870549

Steam railway starting from the Slate Museum, running along lakeside through country park.

National Slate Museum W

Padarn Country Park
LL55 4TY

☎ 01286 870630

In the former workshops of Dinorwig Quarry, showing much of the original machinery and equipment used. Films and slides of quarry work.

Padarn Country Park

LL55 4TY

☎ 01286 870892

On shore of the lake with native oak trees and walks through quarry remains.

Piggery Pottery W

Cwm y Glo, Nr Llanberis LL55 4DA

☎ 01286 871931

Pottery Workshops. Children welcome.

Snowdon Mountain Railway W

Llanberis LL55 4TY

☎ 0871 720 0033

Runs a regular passenger service to the summit of Snowdon using steam powered rack-and-pinion locomotives.

Snowdon Sherpa Bus Service

☎ 0870 6082608

www.gwynedd.uk/bws

The Sherpa Bus Service allows you to leave the car behind and use their comprehensive bus network. Open-top buses in summer.

Betws-y-coed Area

Capel Garmon

Burial chamber with remains of long barrow. North of A5 (between Betws-y-Coed & Llanrwst), follow signs to Capel Garmon.

Conwy Falls

Nr Penmachno LL24 0PD

☎ 01690 710696

Conwy Valley Railway Museum W

LL24 0AL

☎ 01690 710568

Housed in a purpose-built building adjacent to the station, with many items showing all aspects of railway life.

National Park Visitor Centre W

Large and colourful exhibition on Snowdonia. Children's room, information desk, slide presentations and craft displays.

Swallow Falls

Betws-y-coed
☎ 01490 420486
Good views of tumbling cataract just by the A5 above the village.

Waterloo Bridge

Built in the same year as the Battle of Waterloo, a superb cast iron bridge carrying the A5 over the river.

Beddgelert Area

Gelert's Grave

A short walk along the riverbank to legendary grave that gave the village its name.

Short or long walks

in beautiful surroundings, particularly along the river.

Sygun Copper Mine   W

On the A498 Beddgelert Road to Capel Curig. LL55 4NE
☎ 01766 890595
Guided tours around nineteenth-century copper mine and caves with views of Gwynant Valley. Visitor Centre on site.

Cycling & Mountain Biking

Beddgelert Bikes

Beddgelert Forest LL55 4UU
Bike hire service
☎ 01766 890434

Beics Betws

Betws-y-Coed LL24 0AB
☎ 01690 710766

Beics Menai

Slate Quay, Caernarfon LL55 2pb
☎ 01286 676804

Gwydir Forest Mountain Biking

☎ 01492 641707 ex 235

Snowdonia Cycle Hire

☎ 01492 878771

Tyred Out

Penmachno LL24 0PU
☎ 01690 710181

A Taste of Walks

☎ 08450 103300
Each year the True Taste Walks Food & Drink awards are given to walks; top food and drink producers and best places to eat out. Call for more information.

In stunning contrast to the mountains of Snowdonia is the Lleyn peninsula to the west, stretching like a long finger towards Ireland. Some 25 miles (40 km) long and between 5 and 10 miles (8 and 16 km) wide it is an area of outstanding beauty and given the more temperate weather it is accustomed to, can compare with any coastline throughout Europe.

It is a land of rolling scenery, dark hills and beautiful coves and beaches. Despite the influx of visitors in summer it has retained its Welsh charm and language. Close to the hills and well provided with facilities for the visitor it can be an ideal base for touring or for those who enjoy a relaxed holiday but occasionally like a good day on the hills. With easy access to the beaches and bays it will suit the boating enthusiast, the fisherman and children who enjoy exploring rock pools. There are cliffs for the climber, bird watcher and botanist and golf courses for those who enjoy more athletic pursuits.

Divided from the bulk of Snowdonia by a range of hills of grand stature but limited height it has much to occupy the visitor. For those who like to explore the landscape this area is steeped in history both prehistoric and from the more recent Celtic period. Walkers can enjoy the sharp hills or a

coastal jaunt. All around there is a great feeling of openness, the sky seems to dominate all the scenery.

Caernarfon to Tremadog

For convenience, the Caernarfon-Beddgelert-Porthmadog road will be regarded as the eastern boundary of the area. It is a pleasant road ascending gradually from suburban Caernarfon past the old Roman fort of Segontium and following the course of the ancient Roman road into the heart of Snowdonia. Heading south the sharp bulk of **Mynydd Mawr** on the right has the profile of an elephant. Passing below the trunk and along the shores of **Llyn Cwellyn** and the Snowdon Ranger Youth Hostel, once famous for its 'Ranger' who led walkers to the nearby summit of Snowdon, the road arrives at **Rhyd-Ddu**.

Turning right, to the west, leads up to **Bwlchgylfin**, which gives relatively easy access for walkers to this superb range of hills. Close to the summit of the pass is **Llyn-y-Dywarchen**, a diminutive lake that was once one of the wonders of Wales. It had a legendary floating island, which could carry cattle across the lake; visitors came from far and wide to see this spectacle which is sadly no longer evident.

From the top of the pass, a rather gloomy place, the view to the west is one of slate waste and huge tips. What devastation man has created in the pursuit of money! Around the village of **Nantlle** many of these huge craters have now filled with water, but efforts are being made to restore the machinery

and workings of one mine above the village.

For the summit of Mynydd Mawr go north on the path which leaves from the top of the pass and follow it from the western end of the lake near a small building. It rises easily at first through a miniature rocky pass up an easy grass slope until it narrows towards the summit with views straight down to Llyn Cwellyn. The descent is by the same route.

To the south of the pass rises **Y Garn**, a spur of **Mynydd Drws-y-Coed**, the northern most peak of the Nantlle ridge. The traverse of the ridge is an excellent day's walking, covering in all five peaks over 2,000 ft (610 m). The route is not difficult to follow with the aid of a good map and compass, but for many it will be a major expedition and is outside the scope of this guide.

South from Rhyd-Ddu stretches the **Beddgelert Forest**, covering much of the lower slopes of **Moel Hebog**. The Forestry Commission has done much to encourage people to use the forest; there is an excellent camp site and caravan site, a visitor information centre and shop.

From the car park in the forest starts

Go orienteering

Available at the shop is an orienteering map of the forest – for those who have never tried the sport it is an excellent introduction and a good way to spend the afternoon, testing their navigational skills and exploring the forest, but old clothes are essential.

one of several paths leading up Moel Hebog (2,566 ft [782 m]). It is one of the friendliest mountains in the area, with certainly some of the finest views. The path is clear for most of the way, following the stream right up through the forest, until breaking clear just below a small crag on the left. Half way up the crag, and reached by a tricky scramble is **Ogof (cave of) Owain Glyndwr**. Overlooking the valley this cave is reputed to be the hide-out of the Welsh fourteenth-century leader but it is so small and damp that it hardly befits the hero's grandeur. On the same crag, but much easier to reach, is a small hollow in the cliff, which is a disused asbestos mine, though the narrow seam must have proved uneconomic.

The path continues more steeply now to the col, and at a wall one turns left for Moel Hebog and right for **Moel Lefn** (2,094 ft [638 m]), a minor summit that is worth climbing. The summit of Moel Hebog is reached after a steep climb alongside the wall. The views are magnificent: to the north lies the Nantlle ridge; to the east the Snowdon Range and in the distance Moel Siabod, Cnicht and the Moelwyns: south are the Rhinogs and Tremadog Bay; while to the west the Lleyn Peninsula is at one's feet and on a clear day the coast of Ireland can be seen.

One can descend by the same route but it is better to return east-wards down the path to Cwm Cloch farm and Beddgelert and then walk about a mile back to the forest. The route is equally enjoyable if started from Beddgelert, where the path starts just out on the road to Rhyd-Ddu. Cross the river and go up the lane to a farm at Cwm Cloch. A signpost on the end of the barn directs one up the path, which rises easily at first but becomes more steep near the summit.

South of Moel Hebog the lower hills give some pleasant rambling: but as paths are scarce one has to pick one's route carefully. All give excellent views particularly over the reclaimed estuary of **Traeth Mawr** to the south. The estuary of the **Afon Glaslyn**, known as Traeth Mawr, was once said to be the most beautiful in the whole of Wales. It is now about 7,000 acres (3129 hectares) of reclaimed land, and is frequently flooded after heavy rain. It was created by the building of an embankment (the Cob) across its mouth in 1811 by William Madocks MP. At one time the estuary was navigable up to the Aberglaslyn Bridge. Madocks' intention was to create an easy crossing point for traffic to the Lleyn Peninsula in order to open it up for the Irish trade. He also hoped to dry out the enclosed land for farming. His first intention never succeeded. Holyhead was chosen as the main port for the Irish mail; the second has to a certain extent, providing grazing land only.

Madocks built the village of **Tremadog**, and later Porthmadog to be the port for his great plans. Both names have now been converted to the Welsh, so apart from a statue in Porthmadog little evidence remains of his influence on the project. He lived at **Tan-yr-Allt** above Tremadog and the village was laid out to please him. The poet Shelley was a frequent guest at the house and T E Lawrence (Lawrence of Arabia) was born in the village. The village is still of interest to architects and builders as it

Taking on water, Porthmadog

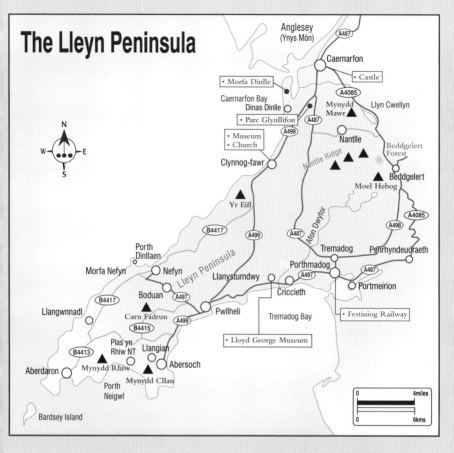

The Lleyn Peninsula

was purpose built to a rectangular plan, its stone houses neatly built on each side of a square. Below the cliffs what looks like a town hall was in fact a theatre, with access from the adjoining hotel on one side, with the cottage at the other end as the changing rooms; it is now a craft shop.

Behind the village, though hidden from the road by woodlands, and stretching for about one mile are **Tremadog Rocks**. They are a favourite area for rock climbing, particularly if it is raining further inland. The woods at the bottom are a nature reserve, much of it being natural growth with native trees.

Porthmadog

Porthmadog was originally planned to be the lesser of the two towns but grew to pre-eminence with the opening of the port. A railway was built across the Cob to the mines at Ffestiniog, so that slates could be exported from the quay. It was intended to be a great cultural centre as well as a port, which no doubt explains why the scheme received the enthusiastic backing of Shelley. The slate trade died when the mines and quarries were closed, so that even the old slate sheds have gone – now replaced by holiday flatlets on the quayside.

103

The railway is still running as the famous **Ffestiniog Railway**, with its terminus on the quayside. The railway, company name still uses the anglicised version of Ffestiniog without the double 'f', was built in 1836 and has the distinction of being the oldest narrow gauge railway in the world. Originally the trucks loaded with slate descended from the quarries under gravity, and the empty ones were hauled back up by horses. It was the first narrow gauge line to introduce steam locomotives, in 1863, and the first to use the 'Fairlie' type of double locomotives, which were articulated in the middle to accommodate the very tight curves. These unusual steam locomotives are still in use as well as a number of more conventional ones. The 13.75-mile (22 km) journey rises over 700 ft (213 m) and there are fine views from the train.

The port has now been taken over by yachtsmen, but because of the silting of the estuary they must choose their sailing times by the tide. Until recent years it was a pleasant little harbour to stroll around, but there is now little of interest, though with the opening of a **Maritime Museum** in an original sailing ship, efforts are being made to revitalise it. The town has a busy shopping centre with many Welsh craft shops to entice the visitor, and a pottery on the outskirts of the town where all are welcome to try their hand.

Several beaches are easily reached from the town centre; the nearest just around the headland is **Borth-y-Gest**, which has fine golden sands and small coves, but bathing is not too safe as the estuary is tidal. Next to it is **Morfa Bychan or Black Rock Sands**, much safer for bathing but more dangerous for walking. This is a two-mile stretch of wide flat beach backed by a large caravan site; car parking is allowed on the beach, but do watch for the tide coming in.

Forcing itself almost into the town centre of Portmadog is the grand little hill of **Moel-y-Gest**, which is a pleasant viewpoint from which to survey the coast. There are several signposted footpaths, which take no more than half an hour to the summit.

Several minor roads leave the main Caernarfon road (A4085) about two miles north of Tremadog. The first goes up to **Cwm Ystradllyn** past the magnificent ruin of a slate mill and then up to a reservoir. Parking is possible at the end of the road, and the hill just to the north is an easier alternative route to the summit of Moel Hebog. The peaceful valley may be explored by following the unmetalled road that continues from the same parking spot, a level walk will bring you to an abandoned slate quarry and barracks. It is a lovely place and not too far to walk, the retaining wall below the slate tip has a superb curve both around and above the trackway.

The road to the north passes **Brynkir Woollen Mills** (open to the public) where Welsh tapestries, flannels and tweeds are woven, and is signposted up to **Cwm Pennant**. This is a beautiful little valley as it winds right into the hills with lots of tumbling streams and places to walk or picnic. It has always been said that this is one of the most beautiful and peaceful of all Welsh valleys. The approach follows a narrow bubbling stream through a rocky defile and then the cwm opens up to a panorama of hills and tranquillity. It is a cul-de-sac, the old coffin road over the col being the only way out at the end of the cwm. It is also possible to reach this valley by turning off the main road at Dolbenmaen just past the castle mound. Halfway along Cwm Pennant, close to a bridge over the stream, a footpath leads across the flat field to the north and uphill through the woods to **Cwm Prysor**, a lovely area in its own right but made even more outstanding by the magnificent **Cornish Beam Engine** which is still in its original position and now renovated. Its history is sketchy but its purpose was to pump the nearby flooded mines clear of water. It does seem totally out of place high up the cwm but somehow enhances the wonderful scenery around it.

Criccieth

Criccieth, the next town along the coast, is a popular resort with several good beaches; the one immediately in front of the town is a good place to launch a dinghy or swim. Above the harbour is the **Criccieth Castle**, only major castle on the Lleyn peninsula and though little remains apart from the gateway it looks impressive from any angle. It is not one of Edward I's castles, being merely enlarged by him on the site of an earlier Welsh fortress. From the castle the views are magnificent and with the well-developed hotel trade in the town it is an excellent centre for touring the peninsula and mountains. Lloyd George, the statesman and Prime Minister, knew Criccieth well, for he spent his childhood in **Llanystum-dwy,** just two miles away. He was educated in the village and died at Ty

Newydd, a house he owned above the Criccieth road. His grave, designed by Sir Clough Williams-Ellis, is beside the river close to the bridge. In the village is a small museum with many mementoes of him.

Shortly after Llanystumdwy, the road divides, that to the north providing a fast route across the Lleyn to Nefyn, while the main road continues to amble down the coast. About one mile after passing a holiday camp (day visitors are allowed), a small signpost directs one to **Penarth Fawr**, an interesting and attractive fifteenth-century manor house. Consisting basically of one large room, it is well preserved and generally fairly quiet.

Pwllheli

Pwllheli, the administrative centre and largest town, is perhaps the capital of the Lleyn. It is an ancient Welsh borough which received its charter from the Black Prince in 1355, and although it now has little of historical interest, with its shops and beaches it is popular with holidaymakers. The town and beach are separated by about half a mile and several centuries, the town being typically old Welsh and the houses along the promenade being a mixture of Victorian and modern. The harbour, protected by a hook of land, which almost encloses it, is safe and, with Gimblet Rock at its entrance, easy to find for both ancient and modern mariners. It is now a marina with a huge selection of yachts moored.

Above: Cwm Ystradllyn with its ruined slate mill and Moel Hebog

Below: Porthmadog Harbour

Beaches on the Lleyn Peninsula

South Coast

Aberdaron

Good beach with safe bathing and boating, last stop for the pilgrims on the way to Bardsey Island. Interesting old church on the edge of the beach. Good headland walks.

Abersoch

Popular seaside resort with miles of fine golden sands. Very popular but still quite charming. Yacht club and mooring facilities, a sailor's paradise.

Criccieth

Two fine beaches divided by castle, safe bathing and launching facilities for small boats.

Llanbedrog

Sandy bay sheltered by headland. Ideal for bathing, boating, fishing and walks on headland.

Near Porthmadog

Borth-y-Gest: Small bays and coves and tidal estuary.
Black Rock Sands: Two miles of good wide sands, safe bathing, drive your car onto the beach. Very popular and backed by caravan sites.

Porth Neigwl (Hell's Mouth)

Open sandy beach about 4 miles (6.4 m) long, plenty of room for everybody.

Pwllheli

Two safe beaches:
Gimblet Rock to south, shingle and sand;
Glandol beach to east, safe and sandy.

North Coast

Edern

Safe bathing, good fishing and boats for hire, power and rowing boats.

Nefyn and Morfa Nefyn

Excellent beaches on wide sandy bays. Popular resorts with bathing, boating and fishing. Golf course on headland. The small village of Porth Dinllaen (along beach or walk over golf course) is well worth a visit, has a pub and a lifeboat station. It is built on the beach.

Porth Golmon (Penllech Beach)

Long stretch of sand with rocks and cliff walks, caves, fishing and good bathing. Interesting church in the village of Llangwnnadl.

Porth Lago

Approached along farm track. Delightful cove, worth finding, a good day out for the whole family.

Tudweiliog

Pleasant beach with fine sands, fairly small but private. Lovely walks along the coast.

Whistling Sands (Porth Oer)

Beautiful bay with safe bathing and unique sands that whistle as you walk across them.

Llanbedrog to Aberdaron

The sand and shingle beaches face south and stretch for almost 5 miles (8 km) to **Llanbedrog** and its rocky point. The bathing is excellent along the whole coastline and once round the headland the beaches continue for several more miles along **St Tudwal's Bay**.

A few miles from Pwllheli along the road to Nefyn is **Bodfuan**, which was the abode of St Buan in the sixth century. The church has stained glass depicting St Cudfan receiving the body of the saint on Bardsey Island. **Bodfuan Woods** were once owned by Ann Boleyn and later Elizabeth I.

Back on the south coast, **Abersoch** is a favourite spot and the small town is now surrounded by caravan sites and holiday homes. It is a delightful little village with a small harbour that has developed in the last twenty to thirty years as the centre for boating enthusiasts in North Wales. With two sheltered bays and wide safe beaches it is ideal for launching and sailing boats of all sizes.

Off-shore islands

Just off the coast are two small islands, no longer inhabited, known as **St Tudwal's Islands**, after the saint who founded a chapel there in the sixth century. Little remains of its Augustinian priory, and the islands are left to the birds and the lighthouse. Boat trips can be taken around the islands, thus also giving the opportunity to view the superb coastline from the sea.

Nearing the end of the Lleyn the villages seem to get smaller and more widely scattered. **Llangian**, near Abersoch, is of some interest as one of the best kept villages in the county and for the sixth-century stone in the churchyard, carved in Latin commemorating Melus, the first mention of a doctor in Wales.

Three miles (4.8 km) south-west of Abersoch is **Mynydd Cilan**, an open cliff-top area with wonderful views, belonging to the National Trust. Then, crossing behind the long bay of **Porth Neigwl or Hell's Mouth**, the road climbs steeply over the shoulder of **Mynydd Rhiw**. The Plas yn Rhiw estate covers 400 acres (162 hectares) and is criss-crossed by tracks and almost surrounded by roads. Rising to 999 ft (302 m) high, it has some pleasant walks with excellent views of the coastline. Early man may have appreciated the hill for the same reason, for there are several archaeological sites to be found on the hillside, including at the northern end a Stone Age axe factory though this is not obvious to the untrained eye. Towards Aberdaron the scenery is superb but somewhat marred by what seems like a forest of telegraph and electricity poles and their overhead lines.

Aberdaron is a tiny village on the very edge of the sea, the last stop for the pilgrims on their way to Bardsey Island. A café and a souvenir shop, **Y Gegin Fawr**, the Big Kitchen, was formerly a hostel and resting place before the crossing, while the small church of St Hywyn, on the very edge of the shore, served their spiritual needs on the last lap. The double-naved church dates from the twelfth to fifteenth centuries. It was built on the site of an ancient Celtic oratory that was founded around the end of the fifth century by Hywyn, who is said to have come from Brittany with Cadfan, the founder of the monastery on **Bardsey Island.**

Braich y Pwll, the headland opposite Bardsey Island, is a fine windswept spot owned by the National Trust. It is a superb place to appreciate the beauty and setting of the island with only the birds for company. It is the most westerly point of Wales and covers 122 acres (49 hectares), including **Mynydd Gwyddel** and **Mynydd Mawr**. Pilgrims embarked here for Bardsey – there was once a chapel here (St Mary's) and it is still possible to find **St Mary's Well**. A steep track leads down to the end of the headland to the site of the old well and departure point for many pilgrims to Bardsey; great care should be taken. A short way north there are walks on the common land of Mynydd Anelog, with fine views across to Bardsey and to Aberdaron Bay.

Bardsey Island

A mile long by half a mile (1.6 by 0.8 m) wide, it had various names in Welsh, but Ynys Enlli, or Island of Currents, as many a sailor and pilgrim will testify, is the most appropriate. Bardsey (a Norse name) was a refuge for monks escaping massacre by the Saxons and has been a place of pilgrimage since the sixth century, becoming so popular that many of the Welsh bishops had their bodies transported and buried there. Little remains of the priory and the later flourishing community, but it is still a place surrounded by myths, mists and legends. Now it is an important centre for the study of birds and is owned by the Bardsey Island Trust.

North to Nefyn

Northwards the cliff scenery is magnificent and there are many fine walks, broken only by the fine coves of **Porth Oer** and **Porth Golmon**. The former is more commonly known as Whistling Sands for the remarkable little squeak given off as one walks on it or runs one's hands through the dry sand. Apparently the quartz grains of the sand are rounded and of uniform size, and when moved, produce a note of uniform pitch. At Porth Golmon it used to be possible to see cows walking down to and along the Penllech Beach at low tide, returning again to their grazing land before the sea came up again, but this unusual practice seems now to have ceased! Near Porth Oer is **Carreg Hall**, once the ancient house of Welsh chieftains, but now engaged in the peaceful pursuit of serving afternoon teas.

From this section of coast the most obvious feature when looking inland is the conical hill which thrusts its way upwards. This is **Carn Fadron** (1,217 ft [371 m]) equidistant between the north and south shores, and the views from its summit are excellent. The hill has innumerable ancient trackways with much evidence of Iron Age settlement, and its exploration provides a pleasant alternative to lounging on the beach.

Near Porth Golmon is the village of **Llangwnnadl**, with its unusual church in a wooded valley running down to the sea. Founded in AD 540 it boasts three naves and three altars. On the south wall is the tombstone of the patron saint (St Gwynhoedl), which is thought to

Criccieth Beach

Tŷ Coch Inn at Porth Dinllaen, which sits literally on the beach

The Lloyd George Museum at Llanstumdwy

Clynnog Fawr Church

Tre'r Ceiri

The site covers about 5 acres (2 hectares) of the hill top. Surrounded by several defensive walls that vary in thickness from 7 ft to 11 ft (2 to 3.4 m) (the inner one still has much of its parapet), it contains the remains of about fifty huts. Though never properly excavated, and unfortunately not under any obvious protection, it is well worth making the effort to see, but on account of lack of care by visitors, it has over the last few years shown a visible deterioration. A Bronze Age cairn of an earlier date can be seen at its north-eastern point.

date from about AD 600. The chalice and paten have been in continuous use since 1574.

Nefyn and **Morfa Nefyn** are the most popular holiday centres along this coast. They both have fine sheltered beaches, ideal for boating and bathing, and, like most of the beaches on the peninsula, have superb views of the mountains, in this case **Yr Eifl or The Rivals**. Lacking pleasure parks and sideshows, these villages are ideal for quiet family holidays, with many guest houses and hotels and with caravan sites nearby.

Nefyn is the larger of the two and was once a major resting point for the pilgrims to Bardsey Island. **Porth Dinllaen**, is a fine natural harbour and its small community can be reached only by a walk along the beach or across the golf course from Morfa Nefyn. It is a delightful collection of beach cottages, mostly holiday homes, and a pub. A gentle stroll at low level around the headland takes one to the lifeboat station and a small sandy beach.

Nefyn, and more particularly Porth Dinllaen, was suggested during the early nineteenth century as an alternative to Holyhead as the major port to Ireland. The defeat of the motion by one vote in Parliament, saved this beautiful stretch of coast for all to enjoy. North along the beach from Nefyn is **Bird Rock**, a craggy headland appropriately named for the many different species found there.

Return to Caernarfon

Continuing along the coast road from Nefyn, the ancient **church of St Beuno at Pistyll** is worth a visit. The corner stone at the eastern end of the north wall is one of only three known to exist. There is a lepers' window on the north side of the chancel and a saint is buried beneath the altar, possibly St Beuno himself. A mural on the north wall is in red ochre and represents the crucifixion, while high on the wall by the altar window is the date 1050 cut into the stone.

Towering above this stretch of coastland and visible from almost anywhere on Lleyn is Yr Eifl, anglicised to 'The Rivals' but meaning The Forks, because of its three peaks. The highest (1,849 ft [564 m]) is flanked on the seaward side by a much quarried summit (1,458 ft [444 m]), and on the inland side by the third peak (1,591 ft [485 m]), surmounted by the ruins of the Iron Age hillfort village of **Tre'r Ceiri**. This site, reached by a steep path from a stile on the Llanaelhaearn road, has the best preserved and most extensive collection of walled huts in the country. What a superb situation for a village.

From this site the summit of Yr Eifl is reached by an easy path that leads from the south end of Tre'r Ceiri down to a shallow valley and up to the highest peak on the Lleyn. The views are extensive – note down at the foot of the mountain, perched almost on the edge of the sea, a small village in a dark valley. This is **Nant Gwrtheyrn**, a tiny hamlet once dependent on quarrying, which can be reached only by foot down a steep and winding road. There is a convenient car park at the end of the road leading seawards from the crossroads in Llithfaen. The descent from the car park on foot for about a mile (1.6 km) brings one to a village of utter peace and quiet without motor cars. The village is simply two lines of cottages set around a square and the inevitable chapel. After lying in ruins for many years the cottages have now been renovated to provide a centre for Welsh language studies. Below is a fine stretch of sandy beach.

The climb back to the car park is a reminder of the plight of the earlier inhabitants and their weekly visit to the shops. The valley is steep-sided and sometimes sombre, the reason perhaps for its other name, Vortigern's Valley. Legend has it that Vortigern, one time British King, took refuge here before being struck down by heavenly fire.

The northern side of the hills is less interesting on account of extensive quarrying around Trefor. On the road to Caernarfon the **church at Clynnog Fawr** is of interest. Founded by St Beuno in AD616, it is one of the finest

Tudor churches in Wales. Until the Dissolution it was a monastery, but the present church dates only from the sixteenth century. It contains many relics of the early saint and he is said to be buried there, it is a surprising church, appearing outwardly to be small but inwardly to be much larger. Nearby is a much older burial site. Close to the shore and just west of the church is an ancient burial chamber with a cap stone about 6 ft)1.8 m) high by 8 ft (2.4 m) long and 5 ft (1.5 m) wide carved with hundreds of cups or depressions.

Several miles to the north of the beautiful church of Clynnog Fawr a minor road turns off to the village of **Llandwrog** and the small resort of **Morfa Dinlle**. The approach to the beach is dominated by a natural hill with the embankments of an Iron Age fort surrounding it. This interesting hillock was almost certainly also used

Parc Glynllifon Historic Gardens and Craft Centre, Caernarfon, Wales best kept secret! (Photo Credit: Parc Glynllifon)

Bardsey from Aberdaron

by the Romans during their occupation and one can only imagine its fascinating history.

Morfa Dinlle has a wide sandy beach with easy access and wonderful views across the bay to The Rivals and Anglesey. At the northern end of the prom-

enade is **Caernarfon Airport**, which offers daily flights over Snowdonia and the surrounding area. The associated **Air World** has a museum of aviation history with displays of planes and helicopters. Those under 10 years old can have fun in the adventure playground.

Beyond the airport is **Fort Belan**, built during the Napoleonic wars to defend the Menai Strait from possible French attack. Lord Newborough garrisoned it with 400 men and equipped it at his own expense – unfortunately it nearly bankrupted him. At time of writing it is privately owned.

Caernarfon is just to the north, and makes a good starting and finishing point for many journeys. To the south stretches one of the finest coastlines and some of the most historic sites in Britain.

Places of Interest & Activities

In & around Porthmadog

Maritime Museum

Borth y Gest LL49 9LU
Porthmadog. Based on the sailing ketch *Garlandstone*, has displays of ships and seamen of Gwynedd. Slate sheds as they used to be.

Porthmadog Pottery   W

Snowdon Street, off the High Street.
LL49 9DF
☎ 01766 512137
Demonstrations of all stages of pottery making, visitors can have a go themselves.

Ffestiniog Railway   W

Porthmadog. LL49 9NF
☎ 01766 516024
Start of steam railway to Blaenau Ffestiniog and also small railway museum and gift shop on the quay.

Tyn Llan Pottery   W

Penmorfa. Displays of crafts and pottery from all over Wales. Snacks and tea available, with picnic spot.
Off A487 north of Tremadog.

Brynkir Woollen Mills   W

Dolbenmaen. East of A487, 5 miles north of Tremadog. LL51 9YU
☎ 01766 530236
Weavers of tapestries, bedspreads and smaller items in traditional patterns.

Welsh Highland Railway   W

Porthmadog LL49 9DY
☎ 01766 516024 (Porthmadog) and
01286 677018 (Caernarfon)
www.whr.co.uk
Tremadog Road, Porthmadog. Steam trains and workshops: trains towards Caernarfon. Extension to Ffestiniog Railway.

Portmeirion Village

Porthmadog LL48 6ET
☎ 01766 772311

Lleyn Penisula

Clynnog Fawr Church   W

On A499 south of Caernarfon. One of the first churches in Wales, dedicated to St Beuno. The rebuilt church is one of the finest Tudor churches in Wales.. Contains many old relics. Close to the church is an old burial site, interesting because the cap-stone is carved with hundreds of cups and rings.

Criccieth Castle

LL52 0DP
☎ 01766 522227

Parc Glynllifon   W

On the A499 south of Caernarfon
LL54 5DY
☎ 01286 830222
One of only 3 grade 1 listed gardens in the county. Second oldest working stationary steam engine in Britain. Craft Centre and café.

Plas Yn Rhiw (NT) W

LL53 8AB

☎ 01758 780219

Small manor house, garden and woodlands.

Shearwater Coastal Cruises

Pwllheli Marina

Bookings through Pwllheli T.I.C

☎ 01758 613000

Glasfryn Activity Park & Bowling Centre W

Pwllheli LL53 6RD

☎ 01766 810202

Includes Karting, quad trekking, archery and coarse fishing

Dinas Dinlle

Off A499, towards Llandwrog about 5 miles (8 km) south of Caernarfon. Oval mound with ramparts and ditch, an ancient defensive spot used by British and Romans.

Lloyd George Museum W

Llanystumdwy LL52 0SH

☎ 01766 522071

Dragon Raiders Ultimate Paintball Park W

Llanystumdwy

☎ 01766 523119

www.dragonraiderspaintball.com

Near Nefyn

Tre'r-Ceiri

By the footpath, leave the B4417 at top of the hill between Llithfaen and Llanaelhaearn north of Nefyn. Britain's oldest walled village. Built on the crown of a hill. Remains of 250 or so stone huts surrounded by several walls. Built about 3,000–4,000 years ago. Worth the effort of seeing.

Nant Gwrtheyrn

Approach only on foot, about 0.75 mile (1.2 km) from car park. Turn off in centre of village of Llithfaen towards the sea, off B4417, 5 miles (8 km) north of Nefyn. Accessible old quarrying village in ancient Vortigerns Valley, on sea side of Yr Eifl. An idyllic spot with small beach. Being renovated as a centre for Welsh studies.

Oriel Plas Glyn y Weddw W

LLanbedrog LL53 7TT

☎ 01758 740763

150-year old art gallery.

Anglesey is the largest island off the coast of Wales and England. Although separated only by the Menai Strait, which vary from several hundred yards to several miles in width, it retains all the character of an island. The climate is generally milder and drier than that of the mainland nearby, making it ideal for seaside holidays. There are many sandy beaches easily accessible for swimming or boating, and safe for children.

The spectacular and varied coastline has been an attraction for many years, much of it now classified as an Area of Outstanding Natural Beauty with many award winning beaches. The great range of beaches can provide the dedicated beach lover with acres of sand or quiet little coves; there are facilities for windsurfing, water skiing and sailing. The cliffs around the island give opportunities for birdwatching and climbing whilst inland there are lakes for fishing and small towns to stroll around. There is a wealth to explore in a relaxed atmosphere.

Compared with the nearby mountains of Snowdonia, the island is flat, the highest point being just over 500 ft (152 m) above sea level. Geologically, Anglesey has some fine examples of ancient rocks, including Pre-Cambrian sandstone and limestone, which come to the surface at several places. The main attraction, however, is its coastline, with its sandy beaches and quiet coves.

Crossing to the island

The Menai Strait are notorious for the tides that rip through them and have

Early history of Anglesey

Many visitors to the island may be aware of its prehistoric connections with the Druids and Celtic Christianity, and later with the Welsh Princes, for legend and fact about the past are inextricably mixed. Perhaps like modern visitors the early settlers found the climate more amenable than the mainland and the nearby mountains. There is much evidence of man's early use of the land, and visitors are today welcomed to the island by the sign 'Môn, Mam Cymru – Anglesey, Mother of Wales'. This title comes from the island's early fertility and farming activity. It was always a major supplier of grain to the rest of Wales, for it was said that more grain was grown in Anglesey, the smallest county, than in the rest of the country put together. There is history to be found throughout the island from prehistoric to Roman to medieval and through to the Victorian era, all easily accessible by car or even bicycle.

always made the crossing to the island dangerous and fraught with difficulty. Today's visitor is more fortunate, for in 1826 Thomas Telford completed his remarkable suspension bridge as part of the London to Holyhead (Caergybi) road, the A5, mentioned in earlier chapters.

Most visitors will arrive by road and cross the Straits over either Telford's wonderful suspension bridge or Stephenson's modified bridge now crossed by the A5. This road bisects the island and has been upgraded to speed you even faster to Holyhead. Looking across from Anglesey with the bridges and Strait in the foreground and the mountains of Snowdonia behind is perhaps one of the finest panoramas in Wales, so do take a little rest and enjoy the view.

The first **Marquess of Anglesey on his limestone column** greets most visitors to the island as they cross the Strait. From high above he surveys his domain and casts an approving eye over the two bridges. Inside there are steps up to a balustrade surrounding the top. It provides a dizzy vantage point from which to survey the island, the Strait and the mountains of Snowdonia, but it is not for the acrophobic. Unfortunately the Marquess never saw the statue, for he died at the age of 86, five years before it was completed.

The A5 crosses the two bridges and runs by the marquess' feet and then turns inland to cross the island. A small diversion off to the south brings you to the best known village in Anglesey. Known throughout Britain for having the longest name is Llanfairpwllgwyn-gyll, or quite simply Llanfair PG. The

The first Marquess of Anglesey

He rose to fame as the Duke of Wellington's second in command at the Battle of Waterloo. As Lord Paget, he had been accompanying the Duke from the battlefield when a cannon ball smashed his leg. 'By God, sir, I've lost my leg' he shouted to the Duke. 'By God, sir, so you have' replied Wellington, and resumed surveying the retreating French. For his bravery at that battle he was created the First Marquess of Anglesey. With his family he lived at Plas Newydd just a mile away and despite his wooden leg he continued to have a successful career in government.

name was further extended to a total of fifty-eight letters by a local wit at the end of the last century, presumably for the benefit of tourists and became **Llanfairpwllgwyngyllgogerych-wyrndrobwllllantysiliogogogoch.** The tiny station has the doubtful distinction of issuing the longest platform ticket in the world and probably also having the longest sign. Many visitors come specifically for this and few will leave without trying to pronounce it. There is a huge **craft shop and visitor centre** adjacent to the station to fill a little more of your time.

By the side of the road on what was the A5 into the village is an octagonal **toll house** designed by Telford. It was the last toll house to operate in Wales, finally opening its gates in 1895, and

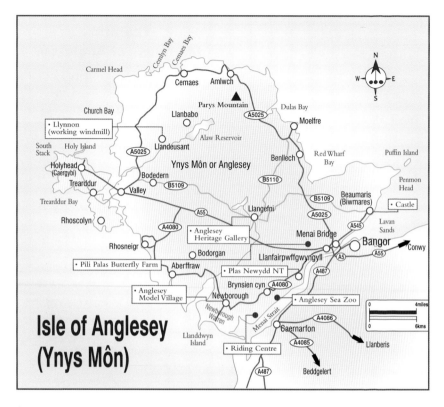

Isle of Anglesey (Ynys Môn)

it still bears the sign stating the tolls. This attractive building is a tribute to the genius of the engineer who did everything so well.

The A5 continues its journey to its destination at Holyhead almost bisecting the island in the process. It is not a particularly exciting drive, for the scenery is fairly plain and the road seems to stretch endlessly in front. Unless one is dashing to the ferry to Ireland or off to climb the sea cliffs on Holy Island it is infinitely more pleasant to take the less busy roads that follow the coast.

The South Coast

It is convenient to start from the An-glesey Column and take the A4080 that runs parallel and just inland from the Menai Strait. After about a mile is the house of **Plas Newydd** between the road and the Strait. One may take the opportunity to relax in the tranquil gardens and take in the magnificent views across the mountains of Snow-donia. Plas Newydd was the home of the First Marquess of Anglesey, the one on the column, and it now has a small museum devoted to his military career with some mementoes of Waterloo.

It was built in the eighteenth century by James Wyatt, and there are some fine rooms, furniture and portraits, as well as sketches, letters and important works by Rex Whistler, an occasional guest at the house, including his largest

The longest place name in the world

Plas Newydd, home of the Marquess of Anglesey (National Trust)

The Romans and the Druids

The south-eastern corner of the island has many similar burial chambers, though none quite as well preserved as Bryn-Celli-Ddu. It does indicate that this was probably the most inhabited part of the island in ancient times. The sea is nearby, the land is flat and it was not as tree-covered as elsewhere. Stories of Druids are well known and give Anglesey a reputation it has never quite lived down. They were not the fearsome people we have come to expect, but the religious leaders of a particular sect, living on the island to escape persecution by the Romans. The burial chambers and cairns in the area probably even pre-date the Druids and are not, as many people imagine, the sacrificial altars of these notorious priests. Though there is in fact very little evidence of their religion or their religious monuments, it is known that this particular corner of the island was their headquarters in the centuries before the Romans arrived

No love was lost between the Romans and Druids, and after a fearsome battle on the very edge of the Straits the Romans succeeded in invading the island. They destroyed everything connected with the religion and subdued the people. It was not until several centuries after the withdrawal of the Romans that Anglesey re-established itself as a religious centre with the coming of Christianity.

wall painting. This huge mural is well worth stopping to examine in detail. Fortunately a guide is nearby to explain its many features and the actual people who are featured on it; perhaps one of its most memorable features is the perspective. Whichever end of this long room you happen to be at, the painted flagstones above the sea wall appear to be laid towards you! Outside, the lawns slope down to the sea wall. During the summer a boat service from the quay at Caernarfon offers trips along the straits to the house, a most unusual approach.

Continuing along the road past Plas Newydd will shortly bring you to the turn off to the chambered cairn of **Bryn–Celli–Ddu**. This is the best preserved of all the burial chambers on Anglesey and is easily accessible on foot from the road. Originally 160 ft (49 m)

in diameter and covering the whole of the area inside the fenced enclosure, little was found when it was excavated in 1928. The stone chamber dates from about 2000 BC but the covering mound is a modern weather protection. From the car park is a gateway to the farm and it is a short walk along the lane to the cairn.

Close by and on the edge of the Menai Strait, almost opposite Caernarfon, is the **Anglesey Sea Zoo**. This marine aquarium has examples of sea life from all round Britain's coast, including some species which are now quite scarce.

Newborough

Newborough, formerly Rhosyr, was built to house the people displaced by Edward I during the construction of

Beaumaris Castle. Recent excavations on the outskirts of the village have uncovered **Llys Rhosyr**, a royal palace of the Princes of Gwynedd. The area beyond and towards the sea, is not one of the busiest parts of the island but it is certainly one of the nicest. From the centre of the village a narrow road goes out to the forest behind the town. There is a charge to enter the forest by road, which gives access to one of the finest beaches in North Wales, with car parks and picnic spots.

The forest is one vast nature reserve covering the sand dunes and salt marshes behind the seashore. Known as **Newborough Warren** for the number of rabbits which used to live there – 80,000 were trapped annually – the dunes cover the old village of Rhosyr and its field system. It is hoped that the trees and grasses recently planted will stabilise the drifting sands. There are several paths and nature trails through the reserve and visitors should stay on the marked paths. An information leaflet is available on the site.

Besides the extensive forests there is a huge beach and foreshore with fine golden sands. It is close to the car park and is never crowded, stretching for several miles in each direction. It is a short walk across the beach to **Llanddwyn Island**, a promontory connected to the mainland by a narrow strip of rock. The island is a nature reserve criss-crossed by easily-followed footpaths. Many wild flowers grow in the grass and undergrowth; visitors are asked to stay on the paths. Birds can be seen nesting around the island's cliffs, and there are superb views of the mainland hills.

On the tip of the island is a light-house and lifeboat station above a small bay. The **lifeboatmen's cottages** have been renovated as a **visitor centre** where there are leaflets giving an outline of the flora and fauna in the area. The adjacent cottages are furnished in original style giving a glimpse of eighteenth-century life there. There are several more miles of beach with **Malltraeth sands** to the north of Llanddwyn Island, all accessible from the car park. The area is a National Nature Reserve and is highly recommended for a fascinating day out.

Until the building of an embankment connecting Newborough with Malltraeth the estuary of the Afon Cefni almost cut the island in half. Now the low lying land is being turned into pastureland, with the estuary on the seaward side of the embankment silting up to create even more expanses of sand at low tide, teeming with wild fowl and waders.

Aberffraw and Rhosneigr

Aberffraw, just beyond Newborough, was for many centuries the capital of Gwynedd and home of the Welsh Princes. Nothing remains today of their palaces, though a Norman arch in the church of St Beuno is traditionally said to have been built by them. The village, a busy port before the coming of the railways, is now a popular holiday centre with some fine beaches and rocky headlands. Accessible at low tide is the tiny church of St Cwyfan, built on a small island. It is thought to have been founded originally in the seventh century but was extensively

Penmon Priory

Menai Bridge

Above: The memorial to Coxswain Richard (Dic) Evans, B.E.M., holder of two RNLI Gold Medals for bravery, at Moelfre

Right: Amlwch Harbour

Below: Red Wharf Bay

rebuilt in 1893.

The bays to the north were the haunt of the eighteenth-century wreckers who lured ships on to the nearby rocks. Today they are popular with yachtsmen and weekend sailors, and some of them are particularly suitable for canoe surfing. **Rhosneigr** stands between two beautiful bays, both excellent for swimming and water sports. It was a popular Edwardian resort, and has remained an ideal family holiday town. The extensive area of gorse-covered dunes just to the north is **Tywyn Trewan Common**, a paradise for bird watchers and botanists.

For those who prefer to watch the creations of modern technology the nearby **RAF aerodrome at Valley** is the home of the RAF advanced jet flying school and the regional centre for the air/sea rescue service. Aircraft and helicopters are coming and going all day long, many on training flights, and there is a car park for plane spotters. The airfield was originally built in 1941 as a terminal for transatlantic crossings for the USAF. During its construction a large cache of bronze weapons and other implements was found in a lake. Known as the Llyn Cerrig Bach hoard, it is now in the National Museum of Wales and is thought to have been votive offerings for Iron Age religious ceremonies.

Holy Island

Across the bay is **Holy Island (Ynys Gybi)**, separated by a narrow strip of water from the main island, and for many centuries the religious centre of Anglesey. Thought to have been the religious stronghold of the Druids, it was settled in the sixth century by St Cybi who built a small church within the remains of the Roman fort at Holyhead. He was a formidable character who travelled the whole of Anglesey converting the people. There is still a church dedicated to him within the walls of the **Roman fort at Holyhead**, but it is a much more recent building with some fine carved stonework. Roman stonework is clearly seen in the walls of the churchyard. The town of Holyhead is still known in Welsh as Caergybi, Gybi's fortress.

Holyhead

Holyhead is a bustling town, which has grown to be the largest in Anglesey. It is basically a seaport servicing the busy Irish ferry boats and the developing trade in container ships. The town surrounds the harbour and is gradually spreading up the slopes of Holyhead mountain. Holyhead is also developing as a yachting centre with a pleasant shingle beach and safe mooring,

End of the A5

It has been difficult to avoid the busy A5 trunk road as it carves its way so impressively through the heart of North Wales, particularly as several of the bridges are so significant in the development of the area and are impressive features in their own right. In Holyhead the road finally reaches its destination and terminates at a triumphal arch on the quayside, just 267 miles (430 km) from Marble Arch in London – a triumph of road building and the foresight of Thomas Telford.

protected by a long breakwater. A promenade, running along its full length, makes it also extremely popular for sea fishermen.

Behind the town, **Holyhead Mountain** rises gently to the low banks of an ancient hill fort of indeterminate age on its summit. Much of the headland is a nature reserve controlled by the Royal Society for the Protection of Birds. The steep cliffs and hillsides are a favourite nesting place for many seabirds including puffins, guillemots, gulls and razorbills. During June and July the rare auk may also be seen there. Perhaps the best place to observe the birds is from the area around **South Stack Lighthouse**.

In a magnificent setting the lighthouse has a true 'Land's End' feel about it. Surrounded by steep cliffs, it can be approached down 379 steps from a car park. They are the best way to see the superb cliff faces around the lighthouse and observe the birds. The rocks offer some of the hardest climbing in Wales for many climbers from the mainland; except in the nesting season they vie with the seabirds for every little ledge and handhold.

The lighthouse is on a small island at the bottom of the cliffs, approached across a small suspension bridge. For the statistically minded the lighthouse is automatic, 91 ft (28 m) high and 197 ft (60 m) above high water, and was built in 1808 by David Alexander, who also built Dartmoor Prison. It used to be open to the public in summer and was probably the most visited lighthouse in Britain, but there is currently no access.

Just below the car park and perched on the very edge of the cliffs is a squat square building that was for many years an ugly ruin. Known as **Ellen's Tower**, it was built in 1868 by the Rt Hon Owen Stanley (MP for Penrhos) as a place to enjoy the view. Recently the Royal Society for the Protection of Birds has converted it into an observatory for bird watchers, for there are fine views of the cliffs. It provides a welcome refuge from the wind for ornithologists and other visitors, who are welcomed.

The whole of the South Stack area is full of interest. Alongside the approach road to the lighthouse is a fine collection of **hut circles**. They are the remains of twenty huts of various shapes and sizes believed to be part of a much larger settlement. Easily accessible from the road they give a good idea of how our ancestors lived, showing signs of their sleeping slabs and hearths. Now in the care of the State they perpetuate in the name **Cythiau'r Gwyddelod, or Irishmen's Walls,** the belief that they were built by settlers from across the sea, although there is no evidence to substantiate this. Nearby are two large standing stones, which are thought to have been the centre stones of a much larger circle, although they now stand alone. Throughout Holy Island there are many other standing stones and hut circles, perhaps indicating that it was after all the centre of religion long before Christianity arrived.

Beaumaris Castle

Moelfre

Red Wharf Bay

Holy Island – southern area

To the south of Holyhead there are several popular holiday resorts, particularly **Trearddur Bay** which sits astride the pre-Telford road to the island. It has several fine beaches with golden sands and rocky outcrops just offshore, making it popular with scuba divers and water skiers, though it can be windy. **Rhoscolyn**, on the southern tip, equally popular for water sports, is more sheltered from the wind. From the village there are some fine cliff-top walks particularly to the **well of St Gwenfaen,** which is reputed to be able to cure mental illness. The nearby cliffs have rock formations showing the bending and folding that took place during the earth's formation.

The west & north coast

Back on the main island of Anglesey the coast to the north with its small bays and rocky coves is very reminiscent of Cornwall. All the beaches give good views across the bay to Holy Island and Holyhead. **Church Bay** is perhaps the most visited beach on that stretch of coast. This north-west corner of the island is dominated by the hill of **Mynydd y Garn**, which, like any hill surrounded by flat land, appears much higher than it actually is. A road runs very close to the top leaving but a short walk to the gorse-topped summit. The views are of the nearby coast, **Carmel Head** and the Wylfa Power Station. Off Carmel Head, **The Skerries** can

be seen, a small group of islets used by breeding birds and seals. The lighthouse on The Skerries has been there since the eighteenth century and was one of the early examples that extracted a toll from every passing ship.

East of the headland the cliffs seem to get wilder until **Cemlyn Bay** is reached. The sheltered beach, once the haunt of pirates, is now a bird sanctuary owned by the National Trust. Visitors are requested to take care during the nesting season (April–June) if they use the cliff top walks around the bay and headland. Much of this northern coast, however, is dominated by the massive bulk of the **Wylfa Nuclear Power Station.** As the power station is in an area of outstanding natural beauty, the Central Electricity Generating Board has provided a nature trail around the headland. There is also an observation tower for looking over the power station and surroundings, while during the summer visitors can tour the site (by appointment).

Several little harbours along the northern coast are worth visiting. The nearest to Wylfa is **Cemaes Bay**; its tiny harbour and pleasant beach are well sheltered from all but the northernmost winds. The cliffs alongside the bay are National Trust property with some pleasant walks, particularly along to **Llanbadrig**. The church above the cliffs is dedicated to St Patrick and is believed to be on the site of one of the oldest churches in Anglesey. It is said that Patrick was shipwrecked on the little **island of Middle Mouse** just a short distance from the headland. He established a church here as thanksgiving for his salvation before leaving to convert the people of Ireland.

Amlwch, a short way further east, has a fine little harbour, built of unmortared rock placed vertically rather than horizontally. It is small and narrow, owing its fame to the nearby **Parys Mountain copper mine**. During the heyday of the mine, it became the main port for the export of copper and the remains of the old quays can still be seen. Ships were built at the port after the decline of the copper industry and the remains of the old slipways can be seen.

Inland from Amlwch are the scarred remains of Parys Mountain. Once the biggest open-cast copper mine in the world, it produced 80,000 tons of ore per year until the early nineteenth century. In the eighteenth century the output was so great as almost to cause the collapse of the whole of Cornwall's great copper mining industry. Visitors must beware of the dangerous shafts and waste heaps around the scattered workings. Efforts are being made to work the mine again, and to show visitors life and conditions in its heyday. The remains are quite dramatic and there is much to see particularly the multicoloured rock.

Further inland, behind the mountain, is **Llyn Alaw**, a fairly new reservoir much favoured by trout fishermen. The church at nearby **Llanbabo** has three grotesque carved faces above the door, while inside is a finely carved slab believed to date from the fourteenth century. There are also several standing stones and burial mounds around the lake. One in particular, known as **Bedd Branwen (Branwen's grave)**, is traditionally the burying place of Branwen mentioned in the Welsh folk legends The Mabinogion.

The eastern side

The eastern side of the island is extremely popular for family holidays. Most of the beaches are well sheltered, with good stretches of fine golden sands and safe bathing. Behind, the countryside is more rolling than elsewhere on the island, with trees more noticeable than on the windy north and west coasts.

Traeth Dulas to the north is a quiet estuary and land-locked bay. Quite out of place are the remains of the old brickworks established in the heyday of Parys Mountain, presumably to cash in on the lucrative building projects. The nearby beaches of **Traeth Lligwy** are excellent, backed by sand dunes.

On the approach roads to the beaches overlooking the bay are several antiquities well worth visiting. They are all signposted from the main road and all can be seen at any time with only a short easy walk. The largest is **Din Lligwy**, probably the fourth-century fortified residence of a native chieftain. Now surrounded by woods it is a fine example, with much of the floor plan and walls evident. On the same walk is **Capel Lligwy**, a church of obscure origin but in a superb situation. Just a short distance along the road is the **Lligwy Burial Chamber**, with an impressive cap stone of solid limestone about 15 ft (5 m) square and 3 ft (0.9 m) thick, supported on a ring of upright rock 'posts'. It was probably erected in the early Bronze Age, about 2,000 BC.

Moelfre, out on the headland, has boats for hire, and, a pebbly beach which is good for water skiing and

Dovecote at Penmon

Festival at Beaumaris (outside the Old Court House museum)

Beaumaris, with the Old Court House in the background

sailing. The lifeboat station has been involved in many famous disasters; perhaps the best known is the *Royal Charter*, which went down nearby with the loss of 452 lives in 1859. To the south, the beaches of **Benllech** and **Red Wharf Bay** are the most popular on the island. They are long and sandy, and at low tide Red Wharf Bay is an extensive estuary. There are several caravan sites along this section of coast.

To the south and stretching out towards the main land is **Penmon Head**, with **Puffin Island** just offshore. Although the coast is scarred by the remains of old limestone quarries, used during the building of both Telford's and Stephenson's bridges across the Menai Strait, the headland is a pretty spot. It can be approached through **Penmon Priory** whose remains, mainly eleventh-century, are adjacent to the road and there is a fine dovecote. Much of the priory is still in use, the abbot's house is still inhabited and the attached church still a parish church. Just behind the buildings is the **well of St Seiriol,** an early Celtic saint active on the island at the same time as St Cybi. Around the well are a few small buildings and the remains of an oval hut, possibly the early saint's cell.

For a small toll you can drive to the coastguard station and café at **Trwyn Du or Black Point** just opposite Puffin Island. It is a grand spot and with the mournful toll of the bell on the lighthouse one can easily conjure up thoughts of shipwrecks. The island, also known as Priestholme or Ynys Seiriol, once had a small monastery, later moved to Penmon Priory, and of course many puffins. The bird population declined on account of the popularity of pickled young birds in the early nineteenth century. At the point, there are some small sandy beaches and excellent views across to the mountains of Snowdonia, particularly the Carneddau. On the south is the entrance to the Menai Strait and across the bay are the **Lavan Sands**, once the main route across the Straits to the island.

Beaumaris

It was to command this route into Anglesey that Edward I built a castle at **Beaumaris**, almost on the edge of the Straits. **Beaumaris Castle** is small compared with its two near neighbours at Conwy and Caernarfon, but around it are the remains of a moat which once connected the castle to the sea. Because of its low lying situation it does not at first sight seem impressive but it is in fact one of the most complete and best designed castles built during Edward's reign. Despite its solid defences it has seen little trouble, a short occupation by the Welsh during Owain Glyndwr's uprising in 1404 probably being the high point of its career. Nevertheless it is a charming little castle, with a children's playground against the outside wall.

Opposite the entrance to the castle is the former **courthouse** built in 1614. Still in its original state, it is furnished as it was built with the coat of arms of James I over the bench and the public

Amwlch port

It has now become a major oil port. At the Anglesey Marine Terminal two miles offshore, crude oil tankers of more than 500,000 tons can moor and discharge their cargo. It is pumped directly ashore and through an underground pipeline to Stanlow, seventy-eight miles away in Cheshire, where it is refined. The harbour has had a new lease of life servicing the terminal and has been expanded, there also is an interesting **mining and maritime exhibition**, detailing the history of the port at the Sail Loft Heritage Centre (tea room available).

area separated by massive iron bars. Until the last century it was the main Assize Court for the county. It was the oldest courthouse in the country and it is said that the notorious Judge Jefferies once held an Assize here. An equally fascinating place for those unfamiliar with the ways of justice is **Beaumaris Jail**. Built in 1829, it still has all the cells, the punishment cell and a tread-wheel unique in Britain. There is much of interest and one is reminded of the harshness of our early penal system.

The town has several other interesting buildings in its narrow streets. The **Bull's Head Hotel**, a favourite with visiting judges is believed to have played host to General Mytton, (Cromwell's general during his Anglesey campaign), Dr Johnson and Charles Dickens. The **church of St Mary and St Nicholas** is almost as old as the castle and has many interesting features. Above the town is the **obelisk memorial to the Bulkeley family**, once the biggest landowners on the island, whose home at Baron Hill is now an overgrown ruin.

Beaumaris plays host each August to the Strait Regatta, a major yachting event organised by the Royal Anglesey Yacht Club. The town has something for everyone: bowls, tennis, fishing, and many elegant buildings and excellent views.

By comparison, **Menai Bridge** seems a busy little town crouching below Telford's suspension bridge.

The **Tegfryn Art Gallery** has regular shows by Welsh artists. Along the **Belgian Walks**, built by refugees during World War I, there are several pleasant walks to **Church Island,** out in the Strait, which is easily reached by a causeway.

Change of status

With the building of the two bridges, much of the importance of the towns along the Strait was removed. Holyhead became the biggest and most important town and **Llangefni**, almost in the centre of the island, took over the role of administrative centre from Beaumaris. Llangefni is a bustling market town with wide streets (market day Thursday), situated on the Afon Cefni by which it could once be reached by boat. There are some easy walks in the vicinity of the town and situated just on the outskirts is Oriel Ynys Mon, which has regular displays demonstrating Anglesey's heritage in a very lively way attempting to bring the past alive.

Most visitors to the island come to see the coastline and the beaches, and will probably spend little time in the interior. There is something for everybody on Anglesey and there is always the probability of warmer weather than on the mainland, so go prepared for a relaxing time but do explore a little, it is well worthwhile.

Puffin Island from Penmon Point

Telford's bridge across the Menai Strait

Beaumaris Castle

Places of Interest & Activities

Menai and the South of Anglesey

Aberffraw

Sandy beach with island church of St Cwfan on site of early Celtic church.

Anglesey Coastal Path

Links 125 miles and 36 coastal villages.

Anglesey Model Village

Newborough LL61 6RS
☎ 01248 440477

Anglesey Sea Zoo   W

Brynsiencyn LL61 6TQ
☎ 01248 430411
www.angleseyseazoo.co.uk
Aquarium with displays of marine animals from Britain's coast.

Beaumaris Castle

Anglesey
☎ 01248 810361

Bryn-Celli-Ddu

1.5 miles (2.2 m) north of A4080 to Llanddaniel Fab, walk up farm track. Best preserved burial mound with huge stones and passage. Probably early Bronze Age.

Brynsiencyn

Many ancient sites around the village including burial chambers and earthworks.

Brynsiencyn Pottery   W

In centre of the village off A4080.

Go Karting

Bodedern
☎ 01407 741144
Open all year.

Henblas Park

Bodorgan
☎ 01407 840440
Family entertainment, displays, tractor rides, farm animals etc. Open: 10.30–5pm, Not open on Sat.

Llanddwyn

Off A4080 in Newborough village. Approach across beach from Newborough Warren. A peninsula of Pre-Cambrian rock, now a nature reserve, with old cottages, lifeboat station and lighthouse. A grand spot for views of the hills across the bay.

Llanfairpwllgwyngyllgogerych-wyrndrobwllllantysiliogo-gogoch   W

Village with the world's longest place name, also the longest platform ticket in the world, available at the railway station souvenir shop. Officially known as Llanfair PG.

Marquess of Anglesey's Column

90 ft (27 m) tall with statue on top commemorating the First Marquess, Lord Paget. Views from platform of mountains and Menai Strait are superb.

Newborough Warren and Malltraeth Sands

Superb beach surrounded by forest

with many forest trails and picnic spots. Access to car park behind dunes (small toll). Signposted from Newborough.

Plas Newydd (NT)   W

Off A4080 two miles from Llanfair PG. LL61 6DQ
☎ 01248 714795
Home of Marquess of Anglesey, with many fine pictures, some by Rex Whistler, mementoes of the Battle of Waterloo. Beautiful grounds.

Pili Palas   W

Menai Bridge LL59 5RP
☎ 01248 712474
Butterfly Park & Childrens' Activities

Rhosneigr

Sandy beaches ideal for bathing and boating. Popular resort with many areas for birdwatching around the village.

Toll House, Llanfair PG

On A5 at start of village. Last to operate, until 1895, still displays tolls.

Valley Airfield

Off A5 before crossing to Holy Island. Car park near RAF aerodrome for 'plane spotters'. Jet trainers and helicopters can be seen coming and going frequently.

Holy Island

Beaches:

Holyhead

Sand and shingle beach inside harbour breakwater (1.5 mile [2.4 m] long).

Rhoscolyn

Sandy beaches with good sheltered bathing. Fine cliff walks.

Silver Bay

Sandy beach near mouth of channel between the two islands.

Trearddur Bay

Fine sands with rocky outcrops, ideal for bathing and many water sports.

Places of interest:

Breakwater Country Park & Holyhead Mountain

☎ 01407 760530 / 762579

Canolfan Ucheldre

Millbank, Holyhead LL65 1TE
☎ 01407 763361
Holiday activities for children. Free

Ellin's Tower (RSPB)

☎ 01407 764973
Bird observatory overlooking South Stack Lighthouse and cliffs, just below the car park for the lighthouse. All the headland is

Cont'd overleaf

W = Suggestions for wet weather

Places of Interest

owned by the RSPB. Care should be taken when walking in the area. Free (Easter-Sep)

Feilw Standing Stones

Penrhos, 1.75 mile (2.8 m) south-west of Holyhead. Two stones believed to be the remains of a larger circle. There are several other standing stones on the island for those interested in these antiquities.

Holyhead (Caergybi)

Roman walls surrounding church of St Gybi, near town centre. Triumphal arch to celebrate completion of A5 and visit of George IV. Busy port for Irish ferries protected by 1.5 mile (2.4 m) breakwater with road along. Ideal for fishing.

Holyhead Maritime Museum

Beach Road, Holyhead LL65 1ES
☎ 01407 769745

Holyhead Mountain Hut Circles

By road to South Stack. Remains of an extensive settlement of second–fourth centuries. Circular and square huts, once thatched. Some have central hearths and upright slabs showing positions of beds and seats.

Penrhos

Off A5 south of Holyhead. Nature reserve with woodlands and sea birds. Nature trails.

South Stack Lighthouse

LL65 1YH
☎ 01407 763207 / 01248 724444
19th Century Lighthouse and suspension bridge. Open: Easter–Sept.

Cont'd overleaf

W = Suggestions for wet weather

Places of Interest & Activities

Along the North & East Coasts of Anglesey

Beaches:

Benllech

Long sandy beach.

Bull Bay

Rocky cove with sheltered bathing and good walks.

Carmel Head

Rocky coves with good cliff walks.

Cemaes Bay

Fine harbour and sandy bay. Good swimming and cliff walks to Llanbadrig and church. Overlooked by Wylfa Nuclear Power Station, hands-on displays, interactive exhibit, which are open to visitors in summer; 10–4pm daily.

Cemlyn Bay

Steep shelving pebble beach, now a bird sanctuary.

Church Bay

Partly sand with rocky outcrops, good views across to Holy Island and Holyhead. Fine cliff walks.

Places of interest:

Amlwch

Small narrow harbour, old port for nearby copper mines of Parys Mountain. Swimming pool in town.

Sail loft Heritage Centre in the Harbour.

Llyn Alaw

Off B5112 at Llanerchymedd. Visitor centre and fishing on reservoir.

Moelfre

Boat hire, sailing and water skiing. Pebble beach.

Parys Mountain

Eighteenth-century copper mines, now a mountain of waste. Some interesting coloured rocks to be seen and industrial archaeology remains, but care must be taken.

Red Wharf Bay (Traeth Coch)

Wide bay with long walk to the sea when tide is out. Good sand and good bathing at high tide.

Traeth Dulas

Land-locked bay with sandy beach. Also remains of old brickworks from heyday of nearby Parys Mountain.

Traeth Lligwy

Sandy beach backed by dunes and fields. Nearby is Iron Age village of Din Lligwy, a short walk across fields to walled village with remains of hut circles, a pleasant stroll. Also Capel Lligwy, a church standing above headland. Nearby is a Neolithic (New Stone Age) burial chamber with massive capstone. All are just by the road, half a mile (0.8 km) north of Llanallgo church.

Along the Menai Strait

Beaumaris Castle

LL58 8AP

☎ 01248 810361

Last of Edward I's forts, once accessible by sea, now well preserved and not aggressive looking. Children's playground next to it.

Belgian Walks

Menai Bridge. Constructed by Belgian refugees during World War I as a promenade. Give good views of Telford's suspension bridge.

Beaumaris Jail   W

Steeple Lane LL58 8EP

☎ 01248 810921

Built in 1829 and still as it was, with treadwheel and cells. All the workrooms, exercise yards and punishment blocks are complete.

Beaumaris Courthouse   W

Castle Street LL58 8BP

☎ 01248 811691

All the original furniture and fittings still intact, very interesting if you are unfamiliar with such buildings. Opposite the castle.

Butterfly Palace (Pili-Palas)
                                            W

Menai Bridge LL59 5RP

☎ 01248 712474

Hundreds of butterflies from all over the world. Exotic plants, nature shop and picnic sites at Menai Bridge.

Church of St Tysilio

On island in Menai Strait accessible by causeway from Belgian Walks.

Llanddona Riding School

Nr Beaumaris

☎ 01248 810183

Penmon Priory & Dovecote

On road from Beaumaris to Puffin Island. Medieval monastery still partly in use as house and church. Dovecote is sixteenth-century with room for 1,000 nests. Good solid stone building with domed roof.

Puffin Island

Along road past Penmon Priory (small toll). Just off Black Point (Trwyn Du), lighthouse with melancholy bell. View of Puffin Island just off-shore.

St Seriol's Well

Penmon. Holy well close to priory with some stone walls possibly of the original saint's cell. About sixth century. Short walk from priory.

Tegfryn Art Gallery

Cadnant Road, Menai Bridge.

☎ 01248 715128

Exhibitions by Welsh artists.

The area of country bounded on the north by the Lledr Valley and the Vale of Ffestiniog, and to the south by Llyn Tegid (Bala Lake) and the Mawddach Estuary contains some of the best, and at the same time the least known mountains of Snowdonia and also some of the finest beaches. The ranges to the north with fourteen peaks over 3,000 ft (914 m) are well known and well visited, but how many people are aware of the quieter slopes of the Rhinogs, the Arenigs and the surrounding hills?

Visitors to this area, either walking or touring, can expect some pleasant surprises. It is a large area crossed by few roads. The hills and moorlands are high, divided by long river valleys bearing the inevitable main road; but the character of the country is such that there are few of these. On the side facing Tremadog Bay are 20 miles (32 km) of beautiful golden sands with some of the best beaches in North Wales.

It must be said that to gain the most from this compact highland area, you must be prepared to get off the beaten track a little. The area abounds with lakes and reservoirs, some easily accessible, others up tiny minor roads that wander uphill far into the mountains. The hills are rough and craggy, and with many ancient trackways into and across them making for some superb walking and mountain biking, any effort will be well rewarded. It is a wonderful area to explore, but do be prepared to be adventurous.

The towns in the area are small, reflecting much that is Welsh – not for them the bright lights and discotheques, but honest down-to-earth service, and the main language of the area is Welsh.

Blaenau Ffestiniog

When the National Park was designated, **Blaenau Ffestiniog**, to the north of this area was excluded. As an industrial town with huge slate tips towering above it, the grey terraces of houses blending in to give it a rather gloomy perspective particularly in the rain, it was considered then to be a blot on the landscape. Now, many years after that decision, the quarries no longer produce slate in any quantity and the once unfavoured town is ironically a popular centre for visitors. It is the slate they come to see, and slate artefacts they come to buy.

The town was known as "the slate capital of Wales" and the evidence is all around. In 1972 Llechwedd, a mine just to the north of the town, began showing visitors around the underground workings. It has now developed into a major visitor centre with tours around the spectacular underground caverns and lakes. It details graphically the hardship of the miners and the huge size of the seams of slate; access is by tramway and there are demonstrations of mining skills throughout the guided tour. A Victorian village has developed around the caverns with shops, a pub and cafés and lots to see and do even if it is raining.

Mines, quarries & trains

For the walker it is possible to visit many of the older disused mines in the hills surrounding Blaenau though care must be taken and shafts avoided. A short distance from the town is **Tan-y-Grisiau**, a small community surrounded by remnants of its slate-mining past. A steep track rises from the back of the village up to the level valley of **Cwmorthin**. It winds easily past **Llyn Cwmorthin**, past a beautifully situated old chapel; and then up to the barracks and sheds of the old quarries (see p.182). The path wanders uphill, to the old **Rhosydd mines**, surrounded by mountains and the highest slate mine in Wales. It is a spectacular setting and it is easy to imagine the hardships of the miner as he walked this path to work at the beginning of each week. In winter it can be particularly bleak. Here all

Slate Quarrying at Blaenau

There are many sorts of mining and quarrying in North Wales, but it is slate for which the region is best known; until recently most buildings had a slate roof. Now with clay or concrete roof tiles, and even imitation slates, there is very little slate mined in the area. Several other towns have been dominated by slate, including Llanberis and Bethesda, but in Blaenau Ffestiniog everything is slate. It has been the life and breath of the community for two hundred years, though now most of the quarries are quiet and the drainage pumps switched off.

Slate underlies most of Snowdonia and appears frequently on or near the surface. Where it does appear it can be quarried, but around Blaenau it was found easier to mine it. Many of the seams are 40 or 50 feet (12 or 15 m) thick and tilted at an angle of forty-five degrees; so the caverns created when the slate was removed are enormous, large enough to contain an average size house.

Undoubtedly life in the quarry was hard; men, usually all from the same family, worked in small groups. They were paid according to their production, and there was no time for idling; they worked underground by candlelight. One man did the drilling to blast the rock loose, sometimes working high above the ground suspended only by a rope around one thigh. The others would break up and reduce the blocks to more manageable sizes, ready for removal. Outside they would be shaped and dressed as required. Each size of roofing slate had its own name: countess, princess, wide lady and many more. It was exported throughout the world and during the great building boom of the eighteenth and nineteenth centuries it is said that Wales roofed the world.

the slate was mined, and the tunnels (or 'adits' as they are known) stretch up and through the hillside.

This is the back of Moelwyn Mawr and a walk up the old inclines or the old tracks through the Rhosydd quarry leads to two great holes from which the slate has been extracted. Just behind these and over the shoulder is a terraced track, which can be followed easily around the hillside to the south to above **Llyn Stwlan**, the top lake of a pump storage scheme. From there a road leads back downhill to Tan-y-Grisiau. The lower reservoir is a favourite place for trout fishermen. This was Britain's first pumped storage hydro-electric power station. On the edge of the lake is **Ffestiniog Visitor Centre** with displays of the role of electricity in modern life and an opportunity to visit the vast underground turbines generating the power.

The Ffestiniog Railway, one of the 'Great Little Trains of Wales', runs between Blaenau Ffestiniog and Porthmadog. Operated now mainly by volunteers, this narrow gauge railway was originally built to carry the slate from the mines in Blaenau to the quay at Porthmadog. These days it provides a regular passenger service for most of the year. The scenery en route is superb, as the track drops from the hills down the beautiful Vale of Ffestiniog before skirting the estuary of Traeth Mawr and crossing the Cob (or embankment) to Porthmadog. It is more usual to catch the train at Porthmadog and do the return journey to and from the terminus near Blaenau Ffestiniog. The little engines are original and excellently maintained. A connecting bus runs up to the slate quarries for visitors.

Vale of Ffestiniog

Near neighbour to Blaenau Ffestiniog is **Llan Ffestiniog**, a quiet little village, standing at the head of the valley to which it gives its name and with superb views of the surrounding mountains. Below, the **Vale of Ffestiniog** is justifiably said to be the most beautiful in North Wales. The steep sided slopes are covered in many places with the original oak woods that once covered much of Wales. The **Afon Dwyryd** meanders lazily along the valley bottom to an ancient stone bridge at **Maentwrog**, a pleasant little village that takes its name from a prehistoric stone in the churchyard – Maen (stone) of Twrog. Now isolated from the sea, the village was once a busy little port for the slate from the surrounding hills. Further downriver adjacent to the roadside are the old quays where the sailing ships would come to load with cargoes of slate destined for Australia, New York and Europe.

Across the valley is **Plas Tan-y-Bwlch**, the Snowdonia National Park Study Centre. Set in beautiful woodlands, the house once belonged to the wealthy Oakley family, owners of the quarries of Blaenau Ffestiniog. The centre runs many courses open to the public on all aspects of the countryside and the National Park. A nature trail starts from the car park by the house and wanders up through the woods to **Llyn Mair**, a small reservoir above, returning eastwards close to the railway and back to the garden. A second trail starts at the lake and circles through the woodland for about three-quarters of a

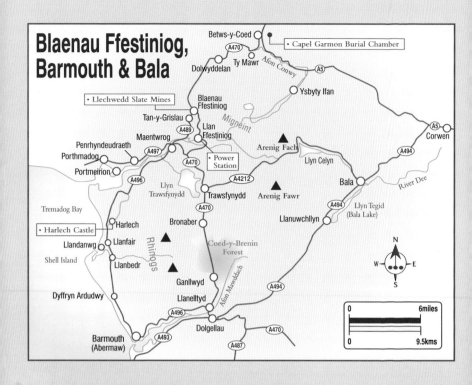

Blaenau Ffestiniog, Barmouth & Bala

Betws-y-Coed
• Capel Garmon Burial Chamber
A470
Ty Mawr
Afon Conwy
A5
Dolwyddelan
Ysbyty Ifan
• Llechwedd Slate Mines
Blaenau Ffestiniog
Corwen
A5
Tan-y-Grislau
Migneint
A489
Llan Ffestiniog
Arenig Fach
Maentwrog
A494
Penrhyndeudraeth
A497
Llyn Celyn
Porthmadog
A470
• Power Station
Portmeirion
A496
A4212
Bala
Llyn Trawsfynydd
Trawsfynydd
Arenig Fawr
River Dee
Tremadog Bay
A494
A470
Llanuwchllyn
Llyn Tegid (Bala Lake)
• Harlech Castle
Harlech
Bronaber
A494
Llandanwg
Llanfair
Coed-y-Brenin Forest
Shell Island
Llanbedr
Rhinogs
Dyffryn Ardudwy
Ganllwyd
Afon Mawddach
A494
Llanelltyd
N
W E
S
A496
Dolgellau
0   6miles
Barmouth (Abermaw)
A493
A470
0   9.5kms
A487

Harlech Castle

mile (1.2 km).

The lake, Llyn Mair (Mary's Lake), is an idyllic spot and can easily be approached by the steep road (B4410), past the Oakley Arms Hotel; there is a picnic area and car park and the rhododendrons are magnificent when in bloom. Just above is one of the stations for the Ffestiniog Railway, which curves and winds its way through the woods of Tan-y-Bwlch.

The river meanders slowly down to **Penrhyndeudraeth** where it is crossed by a toll bridge and then out to sea by **Portmeirion.** This small private village with its tiny harbour was designed and built by the late Sir Clough Williams-Ellis, the Welsh architect whose intention was to create a place free from careless building and advertising. The cottages, mainly in the Italian style, are grouped around a small bay and contain many features collected from other buildings and saved for posterity. The hotel, the centrepiece of the village, is built on the very edge of the estuary; in front is moored a "replica" sailing barque. The village has craft shops and restaurants, and many of the cottages are available to rent. During the 1960s the cult TV series *The Prisoner* was filmed here and there is a small display of memorabilia and souvenirs in one of the cottages. It is on a private estate but visitors are welcome, though charged; access is off the A487 at **Minffordd**.

Harlech

Across the sandy estuary from Portmeirion the hills rise steeply to the lofty summits of the **Rhinog range**. It is a rugged range of hills stretching 20 miles (32 km) to the south, dotted here and there with little lakes and woodlands, penetrated, but never crossed, by single-track mountain roads. It follows the magnificent sweep of Cardigan Bay right down to Barmouth (Abermaw).

At the northern end of the range the coastal land of lowland Morfa Harlech is wide, backed by huge sand dunes and wonderful beaches. The town of Harlech, once a port, stands proudly overlooking the departed sea and backed by the protective hills, the castle perched high on a rocky outcrop dominating the surrounding area.

Built by Edward I in 1238 on the very edge of the bay the castle must have served as a strong reminder to the Welsh of the power of the king, for it is visible for many miles around. (The sea has now retreated, but it is nevertheless striking). It came under attack many times from the Welsh before being taken in 1404 by Owain Glyndwr. It served for some time as his capital before being retaken by the English in 1408.

Men of Harlech

During the Wars of the Roses the Lancastrians held out at the castle for eight years before fleeing overseas. One survivor, a twelve-year-old boy, went on to become Henry VII, and it is said that this siege inspired the march *Men of Harlech*.

It was the last Welsh fortress to be captured during the Civil War, but since then has been left to become a ruin, a grand ruin however, with an inner courtyard surrounded by two mighty walls surmounted by narrow walkways.

There are magnificent views over the estuary, the mountains to the north and the Lleyn Peninsula. The castle must be approached from the town side to gain a full appreciation of the difficulties faced by an attacker.

A short distance to the south of the town in the fields above the road is **Muriaur Gwyddelod** or Irishman's Walls, believed to have been built by settlers from Ireland between 1,000 and 2,000 years ago. The walls are a circular enclosure about 4 ft (1.2 m) high and subdivided into 'rooms'; there are several similarly named sites in North Wales, but we can only guess their true origin. There are many reminders of our prehistoric past in the nearby hills but they must be sought out and they will lead you to some fascinating places.

The beaches along the bay below Harlech are some of the finest; they are backed by sand dunes and are wide enough for the most energetic game of football. Stretching from Harlech Point in the north almost to Barmouth in the south, they are safe for bathing and never crowded. Access to the beaches is from the A496 and is signposted. The Royal St David's golf course lies behind the dunes at Harlech.

The Coast Road

South of Harlech at **Llanfair** are the slate mines of **Charwel** where you can explore the ancient underground workings whilst across the sands on the very edge of the sea is **Llandanwg** (there is a car park right behind the dunes); an interesting medieval church lies half buried by sand dunes nearby. At **Llanbedr** the road to **Shell Island** is over the bridge from the Queen

Victoria Hotel. Take a right turn at the end of the bridge. It goes past the aerodrome and across a causeway, that is covered at high tide. There is a charge to reach the island for day visitors. It is a great spot to collect shells and enjoy the sea, and is ideal for children. It is also a haven for all kinds of wildlife with seasonal influxes of migrating birds in and around the estuary; wild flowers grow in abundance on the dunes.

It is thought that in prehistoric times this particular section of the coastline was the main landing spot for trade with Ireland. There are many old tracks and roadways leading into and across the hills from Llandanwg and Llanbedr. Several tracks can be traced continuously into England. Many of the old tracks, now metalled roads into the hills, are steep and narrow but lead to some fascinating places.

The Rhinogs

One such road leaving Llanbedr beside the Victoria Hotel divides after a mile and a half (2.4 km). The right fork goes up to **Cwm Nantcol**, a beautiful isolated valley below **Rhinog Fach** and **Rhinog Fawr** and a good spot from which to ascend these mountains. The left fork follows the narrow wooded valley of the **Afon Artro** to the head of **Cwm Bychan**, where there is a parking spot by the lake; from here the famous **Roman Steps** can be followed.

The easy footpath leads across the stream and through the woods to the start of the steps, which lead over the shoulder of Rhinog Fawr before descending to the valley beyond. The steps are an interesting walk, particularly if,

Comwell's brother-in-law

Remarkably Col Gwynne Jones was born at Maes y Garnedd 4 miles (6.4 km) up the valley of Cwm Nantcol. From these humble beginnings he went on to become Oliver Cromwell's brother-in-law and signed Charles I death warrant. He was executed after the restoration and is buried close by at **Llanenddwyn**.

at the highest point where there is a small lake, you turn left and walk into the hills to the north; the rock scenery is superb, with huge perched rocks (glacial erratics) sometimes the size of small houses deposited on the glacier-polished granite. The steps are man-made, but there is no evidence that they are Roman. It is more likely that they were a medieval packhorse trail, though the route could very easily be the same as an earlier prehistoric track, which can be traced and followed right through the hills to Bala.

The parallel road which branches off to the south about 1 mile (1.6 km) out of Llanbedr and signposted Cwm Nantcol leads into the very heart of the Rhinog mountains.

There are several interesting nature walks signposted off this road and if you were to park at the very end of the road you would find another paved trackway and more stone steps leading over the pass ahead between Rhinog Fach and Rhinog Fawr. They give reasonably easy access to these hills.

Perhaps the finest road into the hills leaves the coast road from the village of Llanfair. It climbs easily for a mile or two, with several large standing stones beside the road, to the highest point with magnificent views over Harlech, the estuary and the Lleyn Peninsula beyond. The metalled road then dips down to the left around the hillside but directly in front is a rocky track, leading first to an **Iron Age hillfort** that crowns the hill **Moel Geodog**, and then continuing north into and across this range of mountains. There is a possibility that at one time this track was the main road to England from the coast and Ireland, for, though overgrown now, it is terraced into the hillside and paved across the marshes. There are many hut circles and standing stones along the route indicating its importance. If time allows, it makes a good (fairly easy) walk.

The metalled road, which can be followed more easily, runs at a high level parallel with the coast for about 5 miles (8 km) to a small lake. From here a road to the left drops steeply down to rejoin the coast road; or it is possible to continue on this minor road for several more miles and return by the same route. This is a splendid drive though care must be taken as the road is single track with few passing places; it can be joined at several points by climbing steeply from the coast road.

South from Llanbedr the busy road follows the wide coastal plain to **Dyffryn Ardudwy**. Here again there are significant prehistoric remains: signposted next to the school and a very short walk is **Dyffryn Cairn**, which when new was estimated to be 100 ft (31 m) long and 54 ft (17 m) broad. The visible remains are those of the burial chambers and are fine examples of their type.

Joining the A496 just after the village an innocuous minor road to the east leads to further burial chambers and some of the finest old drovers' routes in Snowdonia There are many fine old trackways crossing these hills; almost certainly the road south around the estuary was hazardous and only since the coming of tourism and the railways has access to the coast been opened up. Keen walkers with a map and compass can be guaranteed a splendid day out on these hills, simply by following any of these trackways. They can have the hills to themselves all day with some of the finest scenery in the whole of Wales.

Barmouth

The main seaside resort along this coast is **Barmouth, (Abermaw)** squeezed tightly between the hills and the sea. It owes much of its popularity to the railway and the Victorian penchant for sea bathing, much of the architecture reflecting that era. The railway still plays an important part in the life of Barmouth, approaching the town from the south by an 800 yd (732 m)-long bridge across the estuary. There was a danger that the bridge, which is built on wooden piers, would have to be closed, as it was badly damaged by seaborne rot. Fortunately this has been arrested and for the time being the line has been saved. It has also been passed as fit to take occasional steam trains, which makes a magnificent sight as they cross in this fine setting. The bridge can be used by pedestrians for a small toll and is a recommended way to see the superb views around the estuary.

Between Llanbedr and Cwm Bychan is the lovely Afon Artro

Barmouth

Today Barmouth is still a popular town in a beautiful setting; it has some fine beaches and whether approached by sea, road or rail, the scenery is breath-taking. It remains a traditional seaside resort with a vast beach, a promenade with land train running its full length, an interesting harbour area with a life-boat museum and Sailors Institute and reading room and an old "lock up" on the quayside. On the hillside immediately behind the town and a pleasant stroll above it is **Dinas Oleu**, 4 acres (1.6 hectares) of cliff land and the first property ever acquired by the National Trust in 1895.

It is said that the estuary of the **Afon Mawddach** is similar to a Norwegian fjord with its steeply wooded slopes and surrounding mountains with **Cadair Idris**, grandest of all, looming above all others. The road (A496) to Dolgellau, clinging in many places to the very edges of the shore, is particularly scenic with views across to Cadair Idris high above the opposite bank.

Barmouth to Bala

At the head of the estuary is the very Welsh market town of Dolgellau, a compact little town with narrow streets that seems to be the dividing line between North and Mid-Wales. The grey stone buildings, many made of huge dressed granite blocks seem to be made of the very mountains that surround them. Despite its position and its sixteenth-century bridge, it has figured little in Welsh history. The views to the south are commanded by the mighty summit of Cadair Idris (2,927 ft [892 m]) so it is a good centre for exploring the surrounding hills and valleys, with a number of easy walks in the locality, details of which are available from the Tourist Information Centre.

Dolgellau will be described in detail in the next chapter. Meanwhile, retrace your steps slightly to the small village of **Llanelltyd** to the north-west. Now merely a junction of two major roads it was once the major crossing point of the Mawddach and it was perhaps for this reason that in 1199 a Cistercian abbey was founded on the eastern bank. Little remains of **Cymmer Abbey** nowadays, a few walls and some of the thirteenth-century church but perhaps it was never very large; it does, however, demonstrate what an austere life the monks must have lived and it is a magnificent setting.

A minor road runs up beside the Abbey to **Nannau** where there is a parking area and a signpost pointing to the **Precipice Walk** a delightful circular stroll around the hilltop. Take the kids, take a picnic and enjoy the stunning views of the estuary and the mountains all around, if you only have one walk on your holiday make this it.

North from the abbey the steep-sided valley of the Mawddach is followed on the west by the A470 and on the east by a minor road. Both have their merits as they wind up the wooded valley following this renowned trout river. The 'A' road first reaches the highly recommended **Tyn-y-Groes Hotel**, well known to anglers, while the minor road can be followed into the hills and forests (though a map should be taken to avoid getting lost) where there are some wonderful panoramas. The A470 can be rejoined at **Ganllwyd**.

Extensive forest

This small hamlet is in the heart of the **Coed-y-Brenin Forest**, the Forest of Kings, the oldest and most extensive forest in North Wales. It is also in the heart of the gold prospecting area and though little is found nowadays, at one time the hills and valleys around were akin to the Klondyke.

The best place to learn more of both is to visit the Forestry Commission's **Maesgwm Visitor Centre** north of Ganllwyd, sign-posted off the road at the ancient bridge of **Pont Dolgefeiliau**. It is most interesting, explaining the forest, the wildlife, and for those interested in the history of the area, the gold mining. The displays are well done and explanatory. There is also a splendid display of equipment used in the refining of gold. While there do pick up a leaflet on the forest walks and spend some time exploring. There are marked tracks ideal for walking and mountain biking, and picnic sites throughout the area, many just off the main road. It is a lovely area to visit, but allow plenty of time as there is much to enjoy in the forest.

The map available details over 50 miles (80 km) of roadways and footpaths, but thoroughly recommended is the walk from the car park by the bridge to the twin waterfalls of **Pistyll Cain** and **Rhaeadr Mawddach**. These are not accessible by road but are well worth the effort. Between the two falls is the site of the gold smelting works and above the Mawddach (about half a mile [0.8 km]) is an occasionally-worked gold mine. It is really a splendid area to explore. There are 16,000 acres (6,480 hectares) of forest, mainly firs and spruces but much of the original woodland of old Welsh oaks is intermingled with the new. It is a place of peace, good walking and not too many people.

The road (A470) continues north through the forest and on to the high moorlands, a straight and easy drive allowing plenty of time to enjoy the views before reaching the village of **Trawsfynydd**. The village has achieved dubious fame by being the site of Britain's first inland nuclear power station. Standing on the shores of the nearby lake, the large square structure seems to fit well into the scenery, in many ways enhancing the nearby hills. The Station is being decommissioned at present but there is visitor centre and an opportunity to visit dormant nuclear reactors and control room and see the true impact of it all on the environment.

Historical remains

A short distance beyond the power station a small road goes off to the right under a railway bridge and between steep banks to a wood. Here by a gate are the mounds of a small **Roman amphitheatre**, unique in Wales. It was part of the camp of **Tomen-y-Mur**, visible as a small mound across the field. It must have been an isolated posting for a legionary born and bred in the warmer parts of Europe, especially when the north-westerlies blew in the winter. Nevertheless it was in a fine position and perhaps he could take comfort from the beauty of the surrounding hills.

The main road now drops sharply back into the Vale of Ffestiniog, or turns right through Ffestiniog and Blaenau Ffestiniog to cross the Crimea Pass. The descent into the Lledr Valley is steep, but gives some splendid views of the southern slopes of Moel Siabod. Pass through Roman Bridge, which has no Roman connections, to **Dolwyddelan** and its small castle. Built about 1170 as the home of Llewelyn the Great, the castle has several interesting features,

but is small compared with Edward's fortresses on the coast.

Afon Conwy

The road winds through the Gwydyr Forest to meet and cross the Afon Conwy close to Betws-y-Coed. A short distance upstream from the bridge is the **Fairy Glen and Conwy Falls,** easily approached by a pleasant path along the river bank. Above the falls, the river divides into the Afon Machno, which turns south-west along the lovely **Cwm Penmachno**. Above the village of Penmachno is the little cottage of Ty Mawr, now in the hands of the National Trust. It sits beside a little stream but check times of opening before visiting. It was the birthplace of Bishop William Morgan who translated the Bible into Welsh. Just above the turning to the former Penmachno woollen mill is a car park from which you can visit Ty'n y Coed. This is a small farm in the hands of the National Trust which provides a unique record of the traditional way of life in a Welsh speaking community. Approach the farm along riverside meadows from the car park. The Afon Conwy continues up the valley for several more miles before turning south-west near **Pentrefoelas**.

Leaving the busy main road (A5) the Conwy turns towards its source, followed closely by a minor road. Halfway up the valley is the community of **Ysbyty Ifan**. It was a hospice run by the Knights of St John for the pilgrims on their way to Bardsey Island, but there are now few traces of its past. Four miles (6.4 km) to the south is **Llyn Conwy**, source of this famous river.

Canoeing down the Afon Tryweryn near Bala

The surrounding moorland was until the Dissolution a sanctuary and, despite the many passing pilgrims, was known for its lawlessness. Today the area is equally notorious; known as the **Migneint** it is a marshy plateau with few tracks, crossed only by the roads from Ysbyty Ifan and Penmachno. Close to the junction is an old decorated well which has associations with the pilgrims.

To the south stand the two peaks of **Arenig Fawr** and **Arenig Fach**. The taller, Arenig Fawr, stands to the south of its smaller sister, separated by a road, stream and railway. The now disused railway was the main line from Ffestiniog to Bala and then into England. Running high above Cym Prysor from Trawsfynydd and crossing a high viaduct, which now seems quite out of place in these wild moorlands, it was a magnificent journey under full steam.

The Afon Tryweryn runs towards Bala but was dammed early in the 1960s to form **Llyn Celyn**, which now supplies water to Liverpool. Beneath the waters of the lake was the small community of Capel Celyn, a mainly Quaker village, from where many families left to settle in America with the Pilgrim Fathers. A small chapel and carved rock on the northern shore commemorate the village. Below the dam the river is used for international canoe races, the water level being controlled from the reservoir; it joins the Afon Dee at Bala.

Bala

The town of **Bala** was famous before the Industrial Revolution for its woollen stockings. It takes its name from the Welsh bala, meaning outlet, for there the Dee starts its journey to the sea from the nearby lake. Despite its central position in Wales, at the junction of many old roads, Edward I seems to have found it strategically unimportant. There is a small mound or motte in the town, believed to be of Norman origin though there are doubts even about that.

Modern Bala is something of a holiday centre, reflecting little of its

Methodist upbringing. It stands at the head of **Llyn Tegid or Bala Lake**, the largest natural lake in Wales. It is a favourite spot for yachtsmen as the occasional strong south-westerly wind can give exhilarating sailing. Known also for the fishing, both fly and coarse, the lake yields a unique species called the gwyniad believed to be a survivor from the Ice Age. It is a small fish resembling a herring that spurns the rod and is only occasionally caught by net. There are several specimens in the White Lion Hotel in the town.

The roads on each side of the lake make this shoreline accessible for most of its length, with several pleasant picnic and parking areas off the minor road to the south. A comparatively recent addition along the southern bank is the **Bala**

Methodist origins

It is a grey stone town with a wide main street and was for many years the home of the Reverend Thomas Charles (1755–1814), founder of the British and Foreign Bible Society and a pioneer of Methodism in North Wales; his statue stands in the main street. It continued as a Methodist stronghold when the Reverend Lewis Edwards started an academy in 1837 on the outskirts of the town for young Methodist ministers. Many other Methodists left the town to start a colony in Patagonia in 1865, founding the town of Trelew where the families still live and farm, using Welsh as their first language.

Lake Railway, a narrow gauge railway following the old main line, which has steam and diesel engines running the full length of the lake. The main station is at **Llanuwchllyn** at the south end of the lake. The locomotives once worked the old North Wales slate quarries and ensconced in an open or closed carriage one can enjoy the magnificent mountain and lakeside scenery.

On the northern side of Llyn Tegid the much improved A494 speeds between Bala and Barmouth. For those with more time several metalled tracks across the hills towards Trawsfynydd provide an interesting and adventurous trip. Starting from Llanuwchllyn the recommended route follows the course of the Afon Lliw over to Bronaber and Trawsfynydd. Two miles (3.2 km) up the left-hand side above the road is **Castell Carndochan**, possibly a Norman motte, but more likely the home of an unknown brigand. Nearby are the characteristic white spoil heaps from a nineteenth-century gold mine. The road climbs steeply into the very heart of the mountains following the course of an ancient highway before descending through the forests to **Bronaber** on the Trawsfynydd to Dolgellau road.

It is a wild mountain road passing through some beautiful countryside and forests. Walkers should be armed with the necessary Ordnance Survey maps, either sheet 124 or 125, and a compass. There are few tracks and fewer walkers, and one must be prepared. Please remember also that, though all the hills and countryside are within the Snowdonia National Park, some of the land is privately owned. Walls and fences should not be damaged.

Places of Interest & Activities

Blaenau Ffestiniog, Vale of Ffestiniog and Harlech

Beaches

The whole of the bay in front of Harlech has beautiful golden sands with lots of room for everyone.

Ffestiniog Power Station W

First pumped storage scheme in Britain. Tours of the power station and the top lake are available. Book at the information centre at Tan-y-Grisiau.

Ffestiniog Railway   W

Porthmadog LL49 9NF
☎ 01766 516000
Steam hauled narrow-gauge trains travel 13.5 miles through magnificent scenery to Blaenau Ffestiniog.

Harlech Castle

LL46 2YH
☎ 01766 780552
www.cadur.wales.gov.uk
Fine castle in superb situation. Scene of many bloody battles and inspiration for the march *Men of Harlech*.

Llechwedd Slate Cavern W

Blaenau Ffestiniog LL41 3NB
☎ 01766 830306
Trips inside the slate caverns by tram, and to the deeper caverns by special railway. Demonstrations of slate working and photographs of life in quarries. Slide and photographic displays. Winner of all major tourism awards. Victorian village with pubs & shops. Britain's steepest passenger railway.

Llanfair Slate Caverns   W

☎ 01766 780247
2 miles south of Harlech on A496. LL46 2SA
Walk-in caverns of old slate mine and see the real conditions.

Llys Ednowain Heritage Centre

Trawsfynydd
☎ 01766 770324
Includes info on lake and the power station.

Muriaur Gwyddelod, Irishman's Walls

Situated in fields south of Harlech. Remains of early Iron Age settlements possibly Irish.

Portmeirion

☎ 01766 772311
Off the A487 at Minffordd. LL48 6ET
Beautiful Italianate village conceived by Sir Clough Williams-Ellis. Gardens, café and craft shops. Where *The Prisoner* was filmed.

Plas Tan-y-Bwlch

Maentwrog, on A487. Snowdonia National Park Study Centre, runs courses for visitors on the countryside and aspects of the national park.

Around Llanbedr

Llandanwg Church

Signposted from A496. Ancient church on beach nearly buried by sand dunes. Sandy beach adjacent.

Roman Steps

Turn off at Victoria Hotel in Llanbedr. At head of Cwm Bychan, footpath leads from lake to the steps. Remains of ancient packhorse trail with well preserved steps. Picnic spot at lakeside. Car park charges for vehicle and persons.

Shell Island

Turn off A496 in Llanbedr. Connected by causeway covered at high tide. Sand dunes and excellent beach with café and bars. Millions of shells to collect.

Barmouth and the Mawddach Estuary

Barmouth Estuary

Footpath (toll) across the railway bridge over the estuary gives good views of the estuary and Cadair Idris to the south. Ferry from Barmouth to Penrhyn Point and Fairbourne steam railway.

Coed-y-Brenin Forest and Visitor Centre

Off A470 at Pont Dolgefeiliau. Displays of forest fauna and flora, and gold mining machinery. Plus many tracks of interest in the forest and environs. Very popular with mountain bikers.

Fairbourne & Barmouth Steam Railway

LL38 2EX
☎ 01341 250362
Railway museum round Nature Centre.

Rhaeadr Mawddach and Pistyll Cain

In the forest to the east, follow the footpath from the picnic spot at Pont Dolgefeiliau. Map obtainable at visitor centre as above.

RNLI Maritime Museum   W

On quay in Barmouth. Lifeboat and other ship models, old photographs.

Old Country Life Centre   W

Off A496 at Tal-y-bont. Glimpses of bygone days in the country with traditional tools, crafts, fashions and other aspects. Old mill now houses restaurant and gift shop.

Weaver's Loft

Jubilee Road, Barmouth. Weaving shop producing tapestries and tweed.

Bala

Lake Railway

Llanuwchllyn LL23 7DD
☎ 01678 540666

Cywain Centre

Just west of town on A494. LL23 7NW
☎ 01678 520920
Heritage Centre, Cafe

7. Southern Snowdonia

The southern reaches of the Snowdonia National Park tend to be a little neglected compared with the honey pot areas to the north. It is sometimes forgotten that the Park does in fact stretch quite extensively down to the south of Dolgellau and Bala. It takes in the superb ranges of hills of the Arans and Cadair Idris, the beautiful estuary of the Afon Dyfi and the coastline north of Tywyn to the Afon Mawddach and is easily accessible from Shropshire and the Midlands.

Apart from the coastline with its beaches and resorts, which are always busy in the holiday season, the mountains and the whole inland area tend to be less frequented and less popular than northern Snowdonia. Visitors who do tour the area, however, will be well rewarded; it is a compact area with steep hills and deep tranquil valleys.

The towns and villages are small and typically Welsh; the mountains, which seem to dominate every view, have been described as some of the most beautiful in the country. Certainly this description would fit the Arans, which loom high above the southern end of Bala Lake. The visitor who likes to get a little off the beaten track will have ample opportunity; there are many fine mountain roads that cross high cwms and visit out-of-the-way lakes and valleys. There are nature reserves, quiet rivers and mountain walks. Once into the area the hills are all around, seemingly rolling on forever.

Bala to Dolgellau

At the northern end of the area is Bala Lake and the small town of Bala (see chapter 7), which stands at the outflow of the lake into the Afon Dee. The lake, also called Llyn Tegid, is roughly 4 miles (6.4 km) long by half a mile (0.8 km) wide and lies pleasantly though undramatically below rolling green hills

Southern Snowdonia

with the ever present Arans command-ing the southern view.

The A494 trunk road to Dolgellau follows the northern shoreline before ascending 2 miles (3.2 km) south of the lake to the old farmhouse of **Pont Gwyn** right on the watershed. It is said that a raindrop on one side of the roof runs to the Dee and the Irish Sea and one on the other flows south to join the Afon Wnion and thence to the Maw

and Cardigan Bay.

The **Wnion** flows down a beautiful narrow wooded valley, a land of forest-clad hills and rocky precipices. The road hugs the steep side of the river and the now defunct railway (closed in 1965) fights for space between road and river. It is a lovely journey – British Rail must have sadly regretted closing some of their more picturesque lines. Towards Dolgellau the valley widens marginally and Cadair Idris comes into view over the hilltops, its rampart-like ridges giving it an appearance of strength towering above the valley. After 20 miles (32 km) the river descends to the flood plain and finally joins the broad estuary of the Afon Mawddach and so to the sea. It has been a tossing, tumbling journey through some of the finest scenery in Wales.

An alternative road leaves Bala's main street and crosses the northern shores of the lake, ideal for photographers, and then traverses round the quieter southern lakeside to Llanuwchllyn, home of the Bala Lake Railway which, utilising the old trackway, has regular trips along the lakeside.

A single track road leaves Llanuwchllyn heading almost due south. Signposted Dinas Mawddwy it climbs gradually past the lower slopes of the Arans up the beautiful **Cwm Cynllwyd** to the summit of the pass. This is the infamous **Bwlch-y-Groes**, the highest road in Wales at 1,790 ft (546 m). At the summit is a rather dismal parking area close to the peat hags. It is a bleak spot on a cold day. To the west can be seen the craggy ridge of the Arans. In times gone by the moorlands were famous for the peat gathered for fuel. Apparently some of the best in the land, it was hauled downhill by pony and sledge.

Wild Wales

In 1850, when George Borrow was taking his leave of his host in Bala to traverse this same route, he was warned that his journey that day 'would be very rough over hills and mountains which constituted upon the whole the wildest part of all Wales'. This is still true today. The journey, though more comfortable, is just as awe inspiring in these superb hills.

The Arans, two magnificent peaks, rise sheer to the west, almost twins in shape and height. Formed of a volcanic ridge, which runs between Dinas Mawddwy and Bala Lake, they are the focus of one of the finest mountain walks in southern Snowdonia. **Aran Fawddwy**, the northernmost at 2,970 ft (905 m) and **Aran Benllyn**, slightly less at 2,901 ft, (884 m) are best done as a complete traverse to appreciate their finer qualities. It is easier to start from the northern end close to Llanuwchllyn, where the gradual climb opens expanding vistas with each step. The summit views are unrivalled in Wales: the Berwyns to the east and Arenigs and even Snowdon to the north; Cadair Idris to the west; and to the south a never ending view of rolling hills. The descent recommended would be to follow the ridge south to **Cym Cywarch**, though this does require extra transport; alternatively, return north to where you started the walk.

Motorists journeying south from the Bwlch-y-Groes to **Llanymawddwy** will find their trip equally enjoyable and exciting, though the descent is a trifle worrying for the nervous. Close to the summit is a small, single track road signposted **Lake Vyrnwy** leading off to the east. This is a fine mountain road that gently follows a small stream. There is limited parking but some fine picnic spots in lovely settings. Eventually the bumpy road descends to the lake.

Returning to the Bwlch-y-Groes,

the descent south into the valley is not for the faint hearted. The road is in a superb situation, terraced down the hillside. The hills, craggy and rough with deeply incised streams, give an air of grandeur to this fine cwm. It is a steep and narrow road with few passing places so care must be taken.

Shortly before the valley bottom is reached there is a sharp bend in the road. If you can park here or close by, a small path leads uphill following a fence to **Llaethnant (Milk Valley)** at the very head of the valley. Presumably the name relates to the beauty of the setting. The infant Dyfi flows from the high cwm below Aran Fawddwy over a series of small waterfalls and pools before starting its more leisurely flow to the sea. Some of the pools are ideal for paddling – the valley is sheltered and delightful on a warm sunny day.

At last the road levels out and wanders easily along the valley bottom, first through Llanymawddwy, a hamlet on the Afon Dyfi. Close to the village are some fine waterfalls, notably **Pistyll Gwyn**, a mile to the west along a pleasant little track, which starts by the church. The river is often known as the Royal Dyfi but whether it is because of the magnificent setting or the trout fishing is open to speculation; it is certainly a king of rivers.

Lake Vyrnwy

The lake is in fact a reservoir, opened in 1888 to supply water to Liverpool. It was formed by building a massive dam on a natural ridge across the end of the valley. The old village in the valley, Llanwddyn, was first rebuilt below the dam, then the earlier houses and church were demolished and the villagers evacuated to the new village. Nowadays it is a beautiful setting – the lake formed is roughly 4 miles (6.4 km) long, contains 12,000 million gallons (54,552 million litres) of water and covers 1,100 acres (446 hectares). The area surrounding the lake is a nature reserve, the largest in Wales, and is administered by the Royal Society for the Protection of Birds who have converted an old Calvinistic chapel close to the dam into a visitor centre. There are many marked trails and maps are available of recommended routes.

A narrow road circumnavigates the lake with several picnic spots. Visitors are encouraged, though as the water is for drinking they must beware of causing any form of pollution, so boating and swimming are forbidden. From most viewpoints the Gothic-style draw-off tower gives an almost fairy tale impression to the surroundings. Many of the hillsides have been planted with mixed woodlands, further enhancing the scene and creating natural cover for wildlife and birds.

The lake can also be approached from the village of Penybontfawr in the Tanat Valley. It must be said that no matter what approach is taken, the roads are narrow and care must be exercised.

The toll bridge on the Mawddach Estuary at Penmaenpool

Dinas Mawddwy

There are many tempting places to stop along this tranquil valley before reaching **Dinas Mawddwy**. This small town, which had a fearsome reputation, lies in a lovely amphitheatre below wooded hills; during the flowering season much of the hillside is coloured by a breathtaking display of rhododendrons. The quiet little town, no longer fortified as its name would indicate, huddles along a wide main street and

The bridge over the River Dovey near Machynlleth

The village of Corris, viewed from the A487

was once the centre for the nearby lead mining industry.

Brigands

In the sixteenth century the area was notorious for the red-haired thieves of Mawddwy who terrorised North Wales at that time, plundering, pillaging and killing throughout the land until eventually they were caught in 1555 when eighty of the bandits were condemned to death. Their reputation still lingers however, and amongst this wild scenery it is easy to conjure up the past.

The local pub, **The Red Lion**, has a Brass Room full of old horse brasses and other collectable brass items. Close to the Dyfi bridge just below the village is the terminus of the railway, which closed in 1950. The old engine sheds now houses a **woollen mill** open to the public with a huge craft shop and a display of weaving traditional tapestries; the station building is a café.

To the west of Dinas Mawddwy the busy A470 trunk road climbs up and over the **Bwlch Oerddrws**, with fine views of the southern hills and Cadair Idris before descending to the former old coaching inn of **Cross Foxes** and then down to Dollgellau. It provides one of the main access roads into Wales from Shrewsbury and is a lovely journey through some of the best Welsh scenery.

Mallwyd just to the south of Dinas Mawddwy has a **Brigands Inn**, named to commemorate the Red Robbers. The church, close to the pub, has a whale's rib hanging in the porch (which is dated 1641), dug up locally in the nineteenth century. Its early history is vague, but how it came to be in the area is open to speculation. The church itself is well worth looking in; it is a traditional

167

Welsh church, very simple and peaceful and beautifully maintained.

Around Machynlleth

Still following the Afon Dyfi the valley begins to open out and the hills become less dominant, the road winding easily now through the small villages of **Cemmaes** and **Cemmaes Road** before arriving at **Machynlleth**. To the north of this route is the huge expanse of the Dyfi Forest, which seems to cloak the upper slopes and even the summits of the hills.

Machynlleth, pronounced Ma'hun'hleth, is a smallish market town serving a very widespread population. It has an open atmosphere and a wide main street, at the end of which stands a large decorative clock tower. Built in 1872 to commemorate the coming of age of Lord Londonderry's heir, it is an elaborate structure, which would no doubt cause the planning authorities a headache in this present age.

The Londonderrys lived in a large house, **Plas Machynlleth,** just off the main street, which has been developed since its original foundation in 1653. The gardens are now a pleasant park open to the public.

On the wide main street is the **Owain Glyndwr Institute**, a Tourist Information Centre and library, and adjacent is an older building known as Parliament House which is reputed to be the place where Owain Glyndwr held his first parliament in 1404. It was at this gathering that he first laid down his plans for an independent Wales with its own laws and universities. Sadly for him he never saw his dream come to fruition, though he would doubtless be pleased with the recent progress towards many of his aims.

A small mountain road sign-posted Dylife leaves the eastern end of the main street to follow an ancient trackway, the route of which has changed little. It crosses a golf course to **Forge** before following the narrow valley of the **Afon Dulas** and climbing steeply to pick its way along a series of ridges giving splendid views of the rolling hills all around. To the south is **Plynlimon**, source of many rivers including the Severn. There is evidence of prehistoric man at the high point of the road, and just above is **Bryn-y-Fedwen** with some ancient burial mounds.

From the summit the road descends to the now almost deserted village of **Dylife**, once a bustling township in the eighteenth and nineteenth centuries when over 1,000 people lived here, mining the lead and sending it by horse drawn wagon to Machynlleth. There were three or four inns, several chapels, a church and a school to provide for their needs; now there is one pub, The Star Inn, and a few isolated houses left. During its working life the mine is said to have had some of the best working conditions in the country, but now only a rather ugly site remains.

Above Dylife is a small Roman fortlet which sits atop a rounded hill, again an indication of the antiquity of this roadway and its importance in the past. **Penycroben** hilltop is accessible by a footpath that starts close to the road junction in the village; a right turn along the ridge brings you to the summit and the Roman camp. Little remains to be seen; the walls of the fort were originally turf banks. During excavations in 1960 Roman pots were found, but no evidence to prove that they were aware of the lead ore to be found locally. The name means Gibbet Hill, as later it was used for public executions until the early nineteenth century. The trackway crosses the summit before a right turn returns you to the village.

There are many small mountain roads in this area for those who prefer to get off the beaten track and explore a little but it is also worth returning to Machynlleth and heading north to the **Dyfi Bridge**, built originally in 1533 but later strengthened, to the road junction. The road to the west follows the Dyfi downstream to Aberdyfi and its estuary. For the moment, however, take the northern route up through the valley of another Afon Dulas. This, like most of the roads hereabouts, winds up a narrow wooded valley with steep-sided hills on each side. A minor road runs parallel along the opposite side of the river and gives access to perhaps the most unusual visitor centre in Snowdonia, the Centre for Alternative Technology.

If you can tear yourself away, the Dulas valley still has much in store. There is a pleasant little picnic site at **Tan-y-Coed,** which is the start of a waymarked walk that can be extended to the high moorlands ridge beyond. **Corris**, a small village standing at the confluence of the Dulas and a small tributary and dominated by tips from the surrounding slate workings, is the home of the **Corris Railway Museum**. It houses a collection of

rolling stock (especially their almost unique slate wagons), memorabilia and material relating to the nearby slate quarries and their railways. A length of track has been reinstated.

A minor road follows the Afon Dulas north to **Aberllefeni** giving access to the **Dyfi Forest**. Just short of the village is the **Foel Friog** picnic site, ideal for children and an idyllic spot far from the madding crowd. Close by are several way-marked tracks into the forest. Guides to the walks and the forest can usually be bought at local shops, it is a vast area so do take care not to get lost.

Take the main road from Corris to come first to the junction with the Tal-y-Llyn valley at Minffordd and then climb steeply over the rugged shoulder of Cadair Idris to descend to Cross Foxes and so to Dolgellau.

Aberdovey (Aberdyfi)

The alternative route from Machynlleth and Dyfi Bridge follows the Afon Dyfi, first across the wide river valley and then tightly along the very side of the estuary sharing the narrow bank with the main line railway. The estuary to the south is an important site for the study of wildfowl and migrant waders; the marshes across the estuary are part of the **Dyfi National Nature Reserve** and contain much, beside wildfowl, of scientific interest. Most of the area has restricted access and is maintained by the Royal Society for the Protection of Birds.

Aberdovey is a small coastal resort hugging the side of the estuary. It is

View of Cadair Idris

a colourful little town huddled along the quayside. A venue for yachtsmen and holidaymakers, it still manages to retain its very Welsh feel. The quay is a busy little place catering for the Outward Bound School of Wales who provide courses in sailing, canoeing and climbing locally. Close by is a wide sandy beach which stretches some way up the coast.

Tywyn & Tal-y-Llyn

The road and railway continue to follow the coast past the well-known golf course to **Tywyn**, a rather bleak town that has become a popular seaside resort with a wide sand and shingle beach. Perhaps its main claim to fame is that it is the terminus for the **Tal-y-Llyn Railway**, one of the 'Great Little Trains of Wales'.

The railway opened in 1865 to serve the slate quarries in the Tal-y-Llyn valley. It starts at **Tywyn Wharf** station, where there is a museum with many exhibits from the heyday of narrow gauge railways. Saved from closure by volunteers the line travels inland, skirting the hills and valley of the Afon Fathew for just over 7 miles (11 km). There are several stations en route and at **Dolgoch** the railway crosses an impressive viaduct to the station. A

The water powered mill at Furnace, southwest of Machynlleth

scenic walk to the **Dolgoch water-falls** makes a pleasant excursion, with a not too steep climb up through the woods. The line continues through **Abergynolwyn** to the terminus at **Nant Gwernol**, where there are extensive forest walks.

The narrow valley can also be followed by car, though the journey may be more fraught for the road is narrow and busy in summer. The walks to the falls can easily be reached from the car park by the hotel as can those in the forest above Abergynolwyn. From the village a trackway can be followed to the south up to the old **Bryneglwys slate quarry** for which the railway was originally built.

Continuing up the valley will bring you to **Tal-y-Llyn (lake)**, a pleasant spot with many places to picnic and relax along its shoreline. In fine weather the lake is ideal for swimming and there are two hotels close by. The steep southern slopes of Cadair Idris rise sharply from the lake to dominate the surrounding countryside. The finest ascent of this mountain starts in the valley just north of the lake close to Minffordd, which will be described later.

Parallel with the valley of the Tal-y-Llyn, accessible on the minor road north-west and signposted from Abergynolwyn, is the **Dysynni Valley**; more open and with wider views it has a charm of its own. Dominated by Cadair Idris at its head it is peaceful and more rural, in sharp contrast to its past when it was swept by the great glaciers descending from the north.

Looming large above the lower reaches of the valley is **Craig-y-Aderyn, Bird Rock**, a sharp crag that

On the A458, heading for Mallwyd is the Cann Office Hotel, a 14th century hostellry formerly used for collecting local taxes and on an old drovers' road

is a remnant from the days when this low lying valley was an arm of the sea. It is still a breeding place for cormorants and is protected by the RSPB.

Fairbourne & Creggenan

After a short diversion inland the road from Tywyn towards Dollgellau follows the coastline north and would best be described as a corniche. High above the sea it hugs the steep hillside with some fine views across Cardigan Bay before reaching **Llyngwril** and later **Fairbourne**. Fairbourne, more English in character than Welsh is a small resort of caravan sites and holiday bungalows that, though busy in summer, lie dormant for much of the year.

Fairbourne, like Tywyn further south, is the home of a narrow gauge railway. The **Fairbourne and Barmouth Steam Railway** is a major award winner and visitor attraction; it has been reconstructed to a twelve and a half inch gauge and the trains are pulled by scale replicas of famous narrow gauge locomotives based on both British and foreign prototypes. During the summer a regular service operates along a two-mile (3.2-km) stretch of the coast north to the Mawddach estuary, where an adjoining ferry will take you across the waters to Barmouth before returning. The stations on the line are recreated in Victorian style and much of the equipment is manufactured in the railway's own workshop.

A recent additional attraction at the station is the **Butterfly Safari**. Housed in a purpose-made building are free flying butterflies from Africa, America and Asia. An adjacent collection houses a range of small mammals such as racoons, lemurs and wildcats. Regardless of the weather, the atmosphere is carefully controlled and it can be an ideal family day out. Tickets are available at the station to cover both attractions.

Spectacular waterfall

Below Dylife and just by the road is the **Ffrwd Fawr** waterfall. It is difficult to get a good view and the descent on foot to the base is hazardous but it certainly is the most spectacular fall in Wales. The difficulty of access has ensured that it remains relatively undisturbed. The water drops clear into a deeply incised rocky canyon before pouring over a series of cataracts to the gentler valley below. There is a small viewing platform close to the road but do take care.

A short distance to the north of Fairbourne, close to the wide marshlands of the estuary, is the small village of **Arthog**, its terraced houses hugging the roadside; a single track road climbs steeply from the village past Arthog Hall and waterfalls. Following the stream it rises quickly to reach the twin lakes of **Cregennen** at about 800 ft (244 m). It is a lovely spot, the scenery so different from that of the coast a short distance away. It can also be much cooler. The lakes and the countryside around them were given to the National Trust in 1959 by Major CL Wynne-Jones in memory of his two sons who had been killed in the World War II.

Cregennen sits in a shallow depression below the steep flanks of Cadair Idris; there is a small car park and free access to the banks of the lake. A large log cabin on the shore of the lake was imported from Canada in the late nineteenth century and erected here by the Wynne-Jones family. It can be booked for holidays from the National Trust. It is believed that in prehistoric times the lakes here were considered as holy places and there are a number of Standing stones and cairns close by to prove that it must have been a significant place.

An impressive looking hill, **Bryn Brith** (1,256 ft [383 m]) stands to the north of the lakes, which can be ascended easily by the wide footpath up the ridge. Cadair Idris, which dominates the whole scene, can be climbed from this side, though it must be quite a daunting ascent as the slope here is at its steepest.

Past Cregennen the road wanders around the contour of Cadair giving

The Centre for Alternative Technology

This innovative complex is tucked away in an old slate quarry. It is a demonstration centre showing the possibilities of living on only a small share of the earth's resources with a minimum of pollution and waste. It creates its own energy with windmills and solar panels; it grows much of its own food organically and shows the possibilities of recycling much of the waste we create in everyday living. It demonstrates a more economical way of life both in monetary cost and the saving of the earth's resources. It is altogether a fascinating place with much to offer the visitor in its displays and mode of life. There is a restaurant and bookshop, with free parking; allow plenty of time for your visit you will be truly surprised by the alternatives offered to 'normal' lifestyles.

some fine views of the mountain and also access to several footpaths that lead upwards towards its summit. Passing the small but pleasantly situated **Gwernan Lake** and hotel, it finally descends easily to Dolgellau.

Dolgellau

The main centre and market town for much of the surrounding mountain district, **Dolgellau** can be very busy in summer. Several main roads meet here and at one time all used to pass through the centre of the town, but a bypass now alleviates at least some of this traffic. It is a very Welsh town, despite its popularity with visitors, clustered around its central square with its grey stone and slate buildings.

Despite being the major town in the old county of Merioneth and at the main crossing point of the Afon Wnion it seems to have figured little in Welsh history. In 1405 Owain Glyndwr is said to have held the last Welsh Parliament here, though the house in which it was reputed to have been held was dismantled in 1882 to make way for a shop and

removed bodily to Newtown.

Within a short distance of the town are several shorter walks that have been popular since Victorian times. Perhaps the most famous is the **Precipice Walk**, a three-mile walk which circles **Foel Cynwch** just to the north of the river. The start is best made from near to the entrance of **Nannau Park** on the Dolgellau to Llanfachreth Road, where there is a car park and picnic spot. The route is clearly signposted and follows a terraced route around the hill. It is a delightful stroll, giving some of the best views across the Mawddach estuary and to Cadair Idris in the south. The walking is easy and though airy is safe for children. There are no major climbs involved and if care is taken the path is safe.

Another fine circular walk is the **New Precipice Walk**, which can be completed in about three hours. From **Llanelltyd** take a path to the right over a hump-backed bridge, bear left until you reach a lake, then head towards a house high on the mountainside. This path leads to a mountain road, which drops down to the main road

173

Solar energy and wind display (Photo Credit: Nick Turner/CAT)

at Penmaenpool. This walk also has spectacular views.

The **Torrent Walk** follows the deep glen of the Clydewog, starting at the junction with the Afon Wnion about one and a half miles (2.4 km) east of Dolgellau. Approach down a minor road which leaves the A470 about a mile out of Dolgellau, or alternatively there is a small car park just after turning off to Brithdir, in which case the walk will be downstream. The well made path follows the narrow river as it tumbles down deep clefts and cataracts. It is a lovely walk at any time.

A couple of miles (3.2 km) down-stream from Dolgellau, where a toll road crosses the Afon Mawddach over a wooden bridge, is the **Penmaenpool**

Wildlife Centre in a former railway signal box with an information centre and observation point. The wildlife centre is owned by the Snowdonia National Park, but is administered jointly by the Royal Society for the Protection of Birds and the North Wales Wildlife Trust, who provide telescopes and binoculars for public use.

Tal-y-Llyn Railway

The bells

The town is immortalised in the song *The Bells of Aberdovey* from Charles Dibdin's opera *Liberty Hall*, based on an old Welsh legend that below the sea lies an old village and church, drowned many years ago, but the bells of the church still peal. The legend first appears in the thirteenth century, but became popular with writers in the romantic period of the eighteenth and nineteenth centuries.

When the railway line closed down in 1965 the National Park purchased the section from Dolgellau to Morfa Mawddach and converted it to a walk along the south side of the estuary. For those who like guided walks the RSPB leads groups along the **Railway Walk** during the summer, as well as walks through their bird reserve at **Coed Garth Gell** at the northern end of the Penmaenpool toll bridge.

Cadair Idris

Throughout this area **Cadair Idris** dominates the view. It is a huge mountain that seems to loom above the surrounding countryside no matter where you are. It is one of the great Welsh mountains and though not quite as high as the earlier mentioned Arans it seems to have much more presence. After Snowdon it is perhaps the most climbed mountain in the National Park.

Cadair Idris, the 'Chair of Idris', is named, according to legend, after the giant Idris who was at once astronomer, poet and philosopher. His 'chair'

View of Cadair Idris

Castell-y-Bere

In the isolated Disynni valley, near Abergynolwyn, now far from the mainstream of Welsh political life, Llewelyn the Great built what was to be one of the most important of Welsh castles, Castell-y-Bere. Carefully designed and ornately constructed, it stands on a large promontory of rock near the head of the valley. Begun in 1221, it saw many Welsh rulers, some optimistic some despairing, before Edward I crushed so many hopes in 1277. Dafydd, brother of Llewelyn and the last Welsh prince, established himself at the castle and continued his forays against the English. The enraged Edward sent his armies after Dafydd and the castle became the last point of resistance for the Welsh people. Eventually captured, the castle fell to Edward and was finally destroyed in 1294, its short but turbulent history over. The ruins are rather grand on their rocky crest, and the original layout is still evident with three ruined towers and a rectangular keep. It is difficult to imagine that this peaceful valley played such a significant part in Welsh history.

---

is reputed to be the precipitous hollow between the summit and **Llyn-y-Gadair**, his observatory, a chamber formed by massive rocks. Whoever spends a night in his chair is said to awake as a poet or a madman.

It can only be hoped that Idris is a friendly giant, as the mountain is very popular with walkers; its summit is marked by a huge cairn amongst a chaotic jumble of rocks and the views are superior to those of any mountain in Wales, those to the north being the best. On a clear day it is possible to see the Rhinog range running south to north, and beyond them most of the mountains in the Snowdon massif. To the north-east are the Arenigs and the Arans and further east are the hills of Shropshire, the Long Mynd and the Wrekin; to the south are the Radnor forest and the mountains of central Wales. The whole of the coastline from the Lleyn Peninsula in the north to St Davids Head in the south should be visible on a clear day, and you may

be very lucky and see across the sea to Ireland and the Wicklow Hills. It is certainly a magnificent prospect.

Climbing Cadair

The ascent of this great hill can be made from most points of the compass. Some paths are famous, others less favoured, but all will bring you to the summit with a little effort. Go prepared on this mountain, as there is no railway or summit café to reward your efforts. The paths are reasonably well sign-posted where they leave the road and are quite well worn as they ascend; it is possible in some cases to reach the summit by one of them and descend by an alternative. Those contemplating climbing Cadair Idris should arm themselves with the Ordnance Survey Outdoor Leisure Map No 23 *Snowdonia – Cadair Idris & Bala Lake*, which is excellent and can only increase the enjoyment of their day. They should also allow for at least four hours walking to appreciate the mountain, and go prepared for cooler weather on the summit.

The mountain is in fact a long ridge, precipitous and craggy on its northern face, but more gently sloped to the south. The summit is **Penygadair** at 2,927 ft (892 m). It stands on a narrow section of the ridge high above the cwm or seat of Idris. Llyn-y-Gadair lies to the north and the great bowl of **Llyn Cau** is to the south.

Two famous ascents start from the northern side of the mountain. In Victorian and Edwardian times the **Foxes Path** was popular, starting from Dolgellau and walking along the road, though nowadays most people would opt to park at Gwernan Lake and take the footpath opposite which climbs quite steeply to Llyn-y-Gadair then more steeply up a jumble of boulders to reach the summit.

The **Pony Path** commences close to a car park at **Ty-Nant** about a mile south of Foxes Path. It climbs in a more leisurely way at first, but more steeply as it nears the ridge. Here it meets the path coming up from the south and turns east to climb steeply to the summit. The Foxes Path could be taken as an alternative means of descent.

The very fit might like to contemplate doing the whole ridge, starting at Cross Foxes Hotel in the north and heading south over all the summits to finish on the coast near Fairbourne. It would be a superb walk.

On the southern side of the mountain one of the more popular climbs is the **Minffordd Path**, beginning pleasantly in the valley just to the north of Tall-y-Llyn. A path leaves the roadside close to Minffordd and climbs quite steeply up to Llyn Cau, a haunting spot, a dark lake set in a deep craggy cwm. You can rest awhile now, as the path follows the edge of the lake and is relatively flat before climbing very steeply out and onto the ridge below the summit. An easy but steep ascent leads to the cairn and refuge shelter. This is the best though steepest ascent, full of interest and with some fine situations.

Llanfihangel – a trackway – is the longest ascent, but also the least steep. Starting at the head of the Dysynni valley north of Castell-y-Bere, it ascends easily alongside the Afon Cadair and along the flanks of the hills to meet the Pony Path on the summit ridge. Turning to the east it climbs to the summit. The early part of the trackway follows the line of the ancient pack-horse trail, which continued over the ridge to Dolgellau.

Many keen walkers will doubtless be able to find alternative routes to those suggested. Whichever way you decide to go, it is certain that you will have a memorable day with, weather permitting, one of the best views in the country as your reward.

The whole of the southern section of Snowdonia is in sharp contrast to the rest of North Wales. The scenery is superb, the villages are smaller and more homely and you must to a greater extent be prepared to explore to get the most from the countryside. There is something for everyone, and the effort required is always worthwhile. Every area has its own particular character, each slightly different from its neighbour, but all can be appreciated in their own right and in their own special way.

Places of Interest & Activities

Southern Snowdonia

Butterfly Safari   W
Fairbourne Station
Free flying butterflies from Africa, America and Asia. An adjacent collection houses a range of small mammals such as racoons, lemurs and wildcats.

Castell-y-Bere
Near Abergynolwyn
Rather grand ruins of castle built by Llewelyn the Great.

Centre for Alternative Technology   W
3 miles (4.8 km) north of Machynlleth on A487. SY20 9AZ
☎ 01654 705950
Unique visitor experience which explores alternative ways of living. Discover alternative power sources, green technology and organic methods of growing things. Children's activities and restaurant.

Corris Railway Museum
Corris SY20 9SH
Collection of rolling stock including almost unique slate wagons

Corris Craft Centre
SY20 9RF
Craft shops / Work shops

Cregennen Lakes (NT)
Near Arthog
About 800 ft (244 m) up the twin lakes sit in a shallow depression below the steep flanks of Cadair Idris; there is a car park and free access to the banks of the lake.

Dyfi Forest
Aberllefeni
Foel Friog picnic site, ideal for children; several waymarked tracks into the forest. Guides to the walks and the forest can usually be bought at local shops.

Fairbourne and Barmouth Steam Railway   W
Fairbourne LL38 2EX
☎ 01341 250362
Reconstructed to a twelve and a half inch gauge, trains are pulled by scale replicas of famous narrow gauge locomotives. During the summer a regular service operates along a two-mile (3.2-km) stretch of the coast north to the Mawddach estuary, with ferry to Barmouth.

King Arthur's Labrynth   W
Corris SY20 9RF
☎ 01654 761584
A really good place for kids. Sail on a sub terranean river into the labrynth, Welsh tales of King Arthur re-told in dramatic underground settings. Search for ancient legends in the maze of time. Open: end of Mar–end of Oct, daily 10–5pm.

Lake Vyrnwy
Large reservoir in beautiful setting surrounded by RSPB nature reserve. Visitor centre.

Solar energy and wind display (Photo Credit: Nick Turner/CAT)

Penmaenpool Wildlife Centre

A couple of miles (3.2 km) downstream from Dolgellau.
In a former railway signal box, information centre and observation point, telescopes and binoculars are provided for public use.

Pistyll Gwyn

A mile (1.6 km) to the west of Llanymawddwy.
Fine waterfall along a pleasant little track, which starts by the church.

Ty Siamas, The Magic of Music   W

Eldon Square, Dolgellau LL40 1PU
☎ 01341 421800
Interactive exhibitions,

Tal-y-Llyn Railway   W

☎ 01654 710472
Tywyn to Nant Gwernol
It starts at Tywyn Wharf, where there is a museum with many exhibits from the heyday of narrow gauge railways. The line travels inland for just over 7 miles (11 km). Dolgoch viaduct, scenic walk to the Dolgoch waterfalls, extensive forest walks at Nant Gwernol.

Woollen mill   W

Close to the Dyfi bridge, Dinas Mawddwy.
Huge craft shop, display of weaving traditional tapestries and café in old station building.

Accommodation

There is a great range of accommodation available in North Wales, everything from caravans and guest houses to luxury hotels. Many visitors will have booked their stay in advance, but for those who cannot, or are content to tour without prior booking, many Tourist Information Centres offer a bed booking service. This service is designed to give information on type, style and prices of accommodation and will recommend the most suitable for your requirements.

If you prefer to scout about for your own accommodation the Tourist Information Centres can generally supply a list of hotels, guest houses and self-catering accommodation that is available in the locality. They are listed on p184-85.

going over the mountain pass. They are unlikely to be Roman, but are still very old.

Adventure/Fun Days Out

Plas y Brenin
The National Mountain Centre
Capel Curig, Conwy, LL24 0ET
☎ 01690 720214
info@pyb.co.uk
The complete adventure centre with courses, expeditions and holidays – even sea kyaking

Children' Park (and young at heart)

Greenwood Forest Park
Y Felinheli, nr. Caernarfon LL55 3
☎ 01248 670076
info@greenwoodforestpark.co.uk

Glasfryn Parc Adventure Centre
C. 4miles/7 km out of Pwllheli on A499 to Caernarfon, LL53 6RL
☎ 01766 810202
Go-karting, quads, archery, fishing

Beacon Climbing Centre
Ceunant, Caernarfon LL55 4SA
☎ 0845 450 8222
info@beaconclimbing.com
For the kids and adults too!

Cycling and Mountain Biking
Snowdon area see p.97

Beiciau Madian Quads
Penegoes, Machynlleth SY20 8UW
☎ 01654 702746
Quad biking

SnowBikers
Coed Cae, Taicynhaeaf, Dolgellau, LL40 2TU
☎ 01341 430628
info@SnowBikers.com
Mountain bike training and guiding service

Fishing
See p.184

High Ropes

Get Wet The Adventure Co
Bala
☎ 07909 768950
admin@getwet.co.uk
High ropes adventure/paintballing

Ropeworks
Pwlheli
☎ 01766 819187
info@ropeworks.co.uk

Ropes and Ladders
Gilfach Ddu, Llanberis LL55 4TY
☎ 01286 872310
info @ropesandladders.co.uk
In Padarn Country Park; high ropes
adventure

Tree Top Adventure
Betws-y-coed
☎ 01690 710914
info@ttadventure.co.uk

Mine Exploration

Corris Mine Explorers
C/o Visitor Centre, Corris Craft Centre
SY20 9RF
☎ 01654 761244
info@corrismine explorers.co.uk

Water Sports

Bala Adventure and Watersports
Bala Lake Foreshore, Pensarn Rd
☎ 01678 521059
info@balawatersports.com
Courses and boat hire

Bus services

Sherpa Service

A regular bus service operating around Snowdon during summer for walkers and visitors.
Runs from Caernarfon, Llanrwst or Porthmadog from May–Sept. Timetable from Tourist
Office or Bus Station.
Several bus companies operate within the regions. Timetables are freely available
throughout the region or ring the Traveline ☎ 0870 608 2 608

Cinema

Llandudno Junction

Farmers' Markets

Market days are each month

Northop
Sports Hall, N. Wales College of
Horticulture, CH7 6AA
☎ 01745 561999
9.30 – 1pm, 3rd Sun

Colwyn Bay
Bayview Shopping Centre LL29 9LJ
☎ 01492 680209
9am – 3pm, each Thursday

Conwy
RSPB Nature Reserve
Llandudno Junction LL31 9XZ
(By junction 18, A55)
9am – 2pm, last Wed in month

Dolgellau
Eldon Square LL40 1PS
☎ 01341 450211
10am – 2pm, 3rd Sun

Heritage Highlights

1. Slate

Rhosydd Quarry above Cwm Croesor

2. Castles

Conwy Castle

3. Little trains of Wales

Above: Llanberis Lake Railway

Right: Ffestiniog Railway

Below Conwy

4. Bridges

Corwen
Rhug Estate, LL21 9BD
On A5 west of town
☎ 01490 413221/01691 860 357
10am – 4pm, 1st Sun (May – Oct)

Llanrwst
Ancaster Square,
☎ 01492 651033
9am – 2pm, 3rd Sat

Menai Bridge, Anglesey
☎ 01248 490213
10am, 3rd Sat

Mold
St Mary's Church Hall, King St
☎ 01745 561999
9am – 2pm, 1st Sat

Ruthin
Old Gaol, St Peters Sq
☎ 07798 914721
10am – 3pm, last Sat

Wrexham
Queen's Square, LL11 5DY
☎ 01978 292540
9.30am – 1pm, 3rd Fri

Fishing

In a country so well endowed with rivers, lakes and the sea there is obviously a wide variety of fishing available. It is necessary though to have the required permits for each stretch of inland water. Each small river, stream, lake, reservoir or canal falls within the boundary of the Welsh Water Authority. You must first obtain a licence from them to fish in these waters, then you must obtain a permit (usually available locally) to fish in the relevant stream or lake. Remember the rights to fish any stretch of water belong to the owner of the adjacent bank.

Welsh Water Authority Offices
Gwynedd River Division
Highfield, Caernarfon, Gwynedd
Dee and Clwyd River Division
Shire Hall, Mold, Clwyd
Some lakes for fishing

Llyn Trawsfynydd
Llyn Tegid (Bala Lake)
Llyn Alaw, Anglesey
Tan-y-Grisiau Reservoir, Blaenau Ffestiniog
Llyn Brenig, near Denbigh
Lake Vyrnwy

Sea fishing is widespread right around the coast of North Wales, providing many varieties of fish and fishing. There are sands, piers and jetties and even rocks to provide a variation for the sea angler. Boats can be hired at several centres for the more adventurous.
The keen angler will probably already have a copy of the excellent publication by the Welsh Tourist Board. The Wales Angling Guide available nationally will tell you all you need to know about the inland and sea fishing available throughout Wales.
Coarse Fishing, Glyn Isa, Rowen, Conwy ☎ 01492 650063

Forestry Commission Centres

Bod Petrual

In centre of Clocaenog Forest, 7 miles (11 km) west of Ruthin on the B5105 road to Cerrig-y-Drudion. Story of forest past and present told in lovely setting.

Maesgwm Visitor Centre

In heart of Coed-y-Brenin (Forest of Kings) between Dolgellau and Trawsfynydd. Excellent centre with history of gold mining in the area and natural flora and fauna found in the forest. Lots of walks in miles of forest.

Y Stablau (The Stables)

In centre of village of Betws-y-Coed with information on Snowdonia National Park and the nearby Gwydyr Forest.
Open: daily during Easter week and from Spring Bank Holiday to autumn.

Other Forestry Commission areas worth visiting are:

Beddgelert Forest Park Campsite

Details of walks and wayfaring course within forest available from campsite shop.

Llyn Geirionydd

Off A5 between Betws-y-Coed and Capel Curig.
Picnic site at lakeside. Idyllic spot and start for walks or a cold swim.

Newborough Warren

On Anglesey, off A4080 from Llanfair PG
Superb situation looking across sea to mountains. Miles of beach. Forest located on dunes.

Tan-y-Coed

In Dyfi Forest, just off A487, 4 miles (6.4 km) north of Machynlleth. A picnic site in fine setting with lots of forest walks all around.

Information for people with disabilities

The following organisations can help with planning for your holiday in Wales:

Holiday Care

☎ 01293 774535
www.holidaycare.org.uk

Disability Wales

☎ 029 2088 7325
Fax: 029 2088 8702

Wales Council for the Blind

☎ 029 2047 3954
www.webnet.freeserve.co.uk

Wales Council for the Deaf

☎ 01443 485687
Fax: 01443 408555
Minicom: (01443 485686

Nature Trails & Reserves

There are innumerable nature trails and town trails throughout North Wales. Many are run by local authorities or the Forestry Commission. Most produce individual leaflets containing details of routes, etc. It is therefore wise to enquire locally for these.
The Welsh Tourist Board publishes a booklet available in most shops and information centres, called appropriately Walking, it covers most nature trails and town trails in the area.
The following bird reserves are owned or run by the RSPB (Royal Society for the Protection of Birds) or NWWT (North Wales Wildlife Trust) and welcome visitors. They are usually open.

Aber Oguren

Near Penrhyn Castle.

Coed Garth Gell

Off A496 near north side of Penmaenpool toll bridge across Mawddach estuary.

Conwy Estuary

80 acre RSPB bird sanctuary, off A55.
☎ 01492 584091
Visitor Centre, trails

Reserve and nature trail

Great Orme Country Park
Llandudno
Other nearby reserves at Little Orme, Rhos Point and Pensarn Beach.

Point of Ayr

On the Dee estuary east of Prestatyn.

Llyn Brenig

Clwyd. Off B4501 south-west of Denbigh.

Llyn Penrhyn

Anglesey, near RAF Valley.

Lake Vyrnwy

Information centre off the B4393 Llanwddyn-Llanfyllin road.

Penmaenpool Wildlife Centre

On A493 west of Dolgellau on south side of toll bridge across Mawddach estuary.
Information centre in old railway signal box. Open: daily late May–Sept.

Ellin's Tower RSPB Seabird Centre

South Stack, Anglesey
☎ 01407 764973
Telescopes and remote-controlled cameras at Ellin's Tower Information Centre.
Brynsiecyn, Anglesey

Tourist Information

Bangor
Town Hall, Ffordd Deinol, LL57 7RE
☎ 01248 352786

Barmouth
Old Library, Station Rd LL42 1LU
☎ 01341 280787

Beddgelert
The Old Chapel, LL55 4YD
☎ 01766 890615

Bettws-y-coed
Royal Oak Stables LL24 0AH
☎ 01690 710426

Blaenau Ffestiniog
Unit 3, High St., LL41 3HS
☎ 01766 830360

Carnarfon
Castle St., LL55 1ES
☎ 01286 672232

Colwyn Bay
Imperial Buildings, Station Sq LL29 8LF
☎ 01492 530478

Conwy
Castle Visitor Centre, Castle St., LL32 8LD
☎ 01492 592248

Harlech
High St., LL46 2YA
☎ 01766 780658

Holyhead
Penrhos Beach Rd., LL65 2QB
☎ 01407 762622

Llanberis
41b, High St., LL55 4EU
☎ 01286 870765

Llandudno
1-2, Chapel St., LL30 2YU
☎ 01492 876413

Llanfair PG., Anglesey
Adj. Railway station LL61 5UJ
☎ 01248 713177

Llangollen
Town Hall, Castle St., LL20 5PD
☎ 01978 860828

Mold
The Library, Earl Rd., CH7 1AP
☎ 01352 759331

Porthmadog
High St., LL49 9LD
☎ 01766 512981

Prestatyn
Offa's Dyke Centre, Central Beach
LL19 7EY
☎ 01745 889092

Pwllheli
Min y Don Station, Station Sq., LL53 5HG
☎ 01578 613000

Rhos on Sea
The Promenade LL28 4EP
☎ 01492 548778

Rhyl
Childrens' Village, West Parade LL18 1HZ
☎ 01745 355068

Tywyn
High St., LL36 9AD
☎ 01654 710070

Wrexham
Lambpit St., LL11 1WN
☎ 01978 292015

Index

Index

Published by
Horizon Editions Ltd,
Trading as The Horizon Press
The Oaks, Moor Farm Road West, Ashbourne, DE6 1HD
Tel: (01335) 347349 email: books@thehorizonpress.co.uk

3rd Edition

ISBN 978 1 84306 491 6

Print: Gomer Press Limited. Llandysul, Ceredigion, Wales
Design & Cartography: Michelle Hunt / Mark Titterton
Editor: Helen Maurice-Jones

Front cover: Caernarfon Castle
Back cover, top: Llandudno Bay from the Gt. Orme
Back cover, middle: Chirk Castle and its garden
Back cover, bottom: The longest name of a railway station in the world

Photograph acknowledgements

Steve and Mike Porter, Lindsey Porter, Helen Maurice-Jones,
Robin Eckles, Jim Roberts, and the author. Others acknowledged by the photograph.